BASIC/NOT BORING
MATH SKILLS

SECOND GRADE
BOOK OF
MATH TESTS

Series Concept & Development
by Imogene Forte & Marjorie Frank

Illustrations by Kathleen Bullock

Incentive Publications, Inc.
Nashville, Tennessee

About the cover:
Bound resist, or tie dye, is the most ancient known method of fabric surface design. The brilliance of the basic tie dye design on this cover reflects the possibilities that emerge from the mastery of basic skills.

Cover art by Mary Patricia Deprez, dba Tye Dye Mary®
Cover design by Marta Drayton and Joe Shibley
Illustrated by Kathleen Bullock
Edited by Angela Reiner

ISBN 0-86530-467-X

PRINTED IN THE UNITED STATES OF AMERICA
www.incentivepublications.com

TABLE OF CONTENTS

INSIDE THE
SECOND GRADE BOOK OF MATH TESTS

"I wish I had a convenient, fast way to assess basic skills and standards."

"If only I had a way to find out what my students already know about math!"

"How can I tell if my students are ready for state assessments?"

"If only I had a good way to find out what my students have learned!"

"It takes too long to create my own tests on the units I teach."

"The tests that come with my textbooks are too long or dull."

"I need tests that cover all the skills on a topic, not just a few here and there."

This is what teachers tell us about their needs for testing materials. If you, too, are looking for quality, convenient materials that will help you gauge how well students are moving along towards mastering basic skills and standards—look no further. This is a book of tests such as you've never seen before! It's everything you've wanted in a group of ready-made math assessments for second graders.

- The tests are student-friendly. One glance through the book and you will see why. Students will be surprised that it's a test at all! The pages are inviting and fun. Clever dinosaurs and their Stone Age friends tumble over the pages, leading students through math questions and problems. Your students will not groan when you pass out these tests. They'll want to stick with them all the way to the end to see where the STOP sign is this time!

- The tests are serious. Do not be fooled by the catchy characters and visual appeal! These are thorough assessments of basic content. As a part of the BASIC/Not Boring Skills Series, they give broad coverage of math skills with a flair that makes them favorites of teachers and kids.

- The tests cover all the basic skill areas for math. There are 24 tests within six areas: number concepts & relationships, computation, fractions & money, problem solving, geometry & measurement, and graphing, statistics, & probability.

- The tests are ready to use. In a convenient and manageable size, each test covers a skill area (such as problem-solving strategies, money, geometry, or fractions) that you need to assess. Just give the pages to an individual student, or make copies for an entire class. Answer keys (included in back) are easy to find and easy to use.

- Skills are clearly identified. You can see exactly which skills are tested by reviewing the list of skills provided before each group of tests.

HOW TO USE THE
SECOND GRADE BOOK OF MATH TESTS

Each test can be used in many different ways. Here are a few:

- as a pre-test to see what a student knows or can do on a certain math topic
- as a post-test to find out how well students have mastered a content or skill area
- as a review to check up on student mastery of standards or readiness for state assessments
- as a survey to provide direction for your present or future instruction
- as an instructional tool to guide students through a review of a lesson
- with one student in an assessment or tutorial setting
- with a small group of students for assessment or instruction
- with a whole class for end-of-unit assessment

The book provides you with tools for using the tests effectively and keeping track of how students are progressing on skills or standards:

- 24 Tests on the Topics You Need: These are grouped according to broad topics within math. Each large grouping has two or more sub-tests. Tests are clearly labeled with subject area and specific topic.

- Skills Checklists Correlated to Test Items: At the beginning of each group of tests, you'll find a list of the skills covered. (For instance, pages 10–11 hold lists of skills for the five tests on number concepts and relationships.) Each skill is matched with the exact test items assessing that skill. If a student misses an item on the test, you'll know exactly which skill needs sharpening.

- Student Progress Records: Page 126 holds a reproducible form that can be used to track individual student achievement on all the tests in this book. Make a copy of this form for each student, and record the student's test scores and areas of instructional need.

- Class Progress Records: Pages 127–128 hold reproducible forms for keeping track of an entire class. You can record the dates on which tests are given and keep comments about what you learned from each test as well as notes for further instructional needs.

- Reference for Skill-Sharpening Activities: Pages 129–130 describe the BASIC/Not Boring Skills series, a program of appealing exercises designed to teach, strengthen, or reinforce basic math skills and content. The skills covered in these books are correlated to national curriculum standards and the standards for many states.

- Scoring Guide for Performance Test: A performance test is given for math problem solving. For a complete scoring guide that assesses student performance on this test, use page 140.

- Answer Keys: An easy-to-use answer key is provided for each of the 24 tests. (See pages 132–143.)

THE 2ND GRADE MATH TESTS

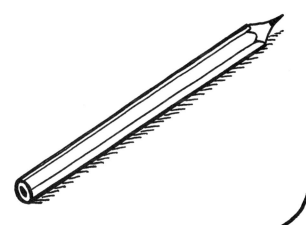

Number Concepts & Relationships Skills Checklists

Number Concepts & Relationships Test # 1:

COUNTING

Test Location: pages 12–15

Skill	Test Items
Read and write ordinals	1–8
Count forward and backward using a number line	9–11
Skip count forward and backward using a number line	12–15
Count forward and backward without a number line	16–24
Use skip counting to find missing numbers	18
Skip count forward without a number line	18, 20, 22, 23
Skip count backward without a number line	19, 21, 24
Use skip counting to solve problems	25

Number Concepts & Relationships Test # 2:

READING & WRITING NUMBERS

Test Location: pages 16–19

Skill	Test Items
Match numerals to number words	1–8
Write numerals to match number words	9–12
Identify correct word name for a numeral	13–15
Write the correct word name for a numeral	16–21
Match large numbers to their word names	22–25

Second Grade Book of Math Tests

NUMBER CONCEPTS

Test Location: pages 20–23

Skill	Test Items
Identify even and odd numbers	1, 2
Match a number to its expanded notation	3–5
Identify place value to hundreds	6–9
Round numbers to the nearest 10	10–17
Round numbers to the nearest 100	18–23
Estimate number amounts	24–30

Number Concepts & Relationships Test # 4:

PLACE VALUE

Test Location: pages 24–27

Skill	Test Items
Identify the place values (up to four digits) in numbers	1–8
Identify the exact place value of digits in a number (up to 4 digits)	5–8
Identify a digit in a particular place value	9–11
Write numbers that have specific values in the ones, tens, hundreds, or thousands places	12–21
Write numbers that have prescribed values for various places from ones through thousands	22–25

Number Concepts & Relationships Test # 5:

NUMBER RELATIONSHIPS

Test Location: pages 28–31

Skill	Test Items
Describe number locations and relationships on a number line	1–3
Identify the smallest or largest number in a group	4–5
Use words to compare two numbers	6–10
Use symbols to compare two numbers	11–14
Write numbers in order from smallest to largest	15–17
Write and compare amounts represented by numbers	18–19
Write numbers described by a relationship to another number	20–22
Determine whether number amounts make sense	23–25

Counting

Name _____

Date _____

Possible Correct Answers: 25

Your Correct Answers: _____

Look at the picture. Use the picture to solve problems 1–8.

ROCK-LIFTING CONTEST TICKETS $2.00

1. Where is Rocky in the line?
   (Circle one.)

   second   fourth

   fifth   seventh

2. Is Fuzzy sixth in line?_____

3. Is Terra seventh in line?_____

4. Who is third in line?

   _____

5. Where is Brock in the line?

   _____

6. Where is Rap in the line?

   _____

7. Who is fifth in line?

   _____

8. Who is second in line?

   _____

Use the number lines to help you answer questions 9–11

9. Brock begins at 7 on the number line. He crawls forward 6 and rests. Then he crawls forward 4. Where does he stop?_____

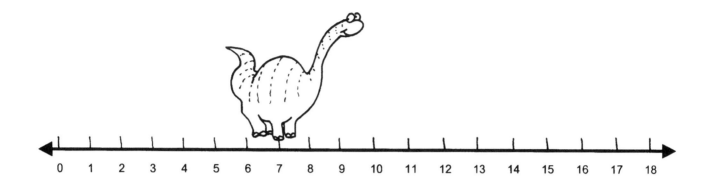

10. Trixie begins at 42. She hops backward 9 and rests. Then she hops forward 5. Where does she stop?_____

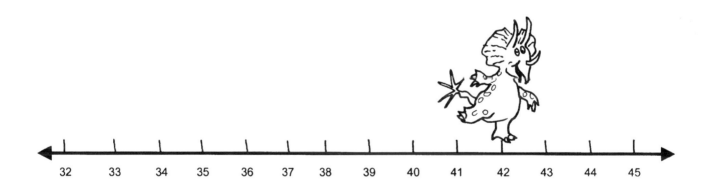

11. Terra begins at 53. She flies forward 7 and rests. Then she flies forward 3. Where does she stop?_____

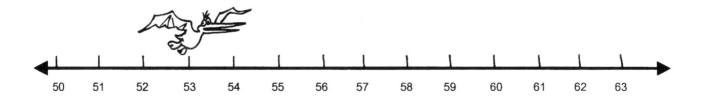

Name _____

13

Use the number lines to help you answer questions 12–15.

12. Rap begins at 102. He runs backward 6 and rests.
Then he runs forward 11. Where does he stop?_____

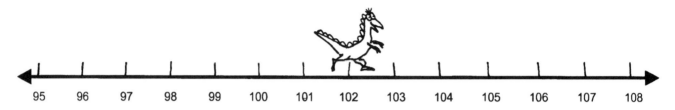

13. Fish begins at 10. He leaps 5 yards at a time.
Fish leaps forward 4 times. Where does he stop?_____

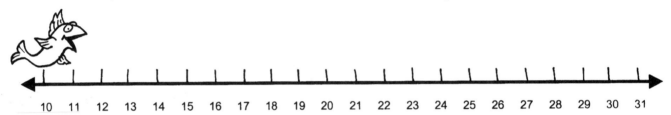

14. Stella begins at 180. She crawls 10 yards at a time.
She crawls 6 times backward. Where does she stop?_____

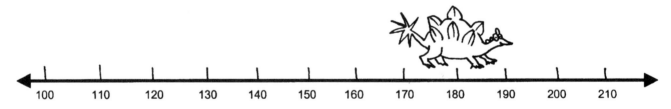

15. Turtle begins at 70. She crawls 2 feet before each rest.
She crawls forward 7 times.
Then she crawls backward 4 times. Where does she stop?_____

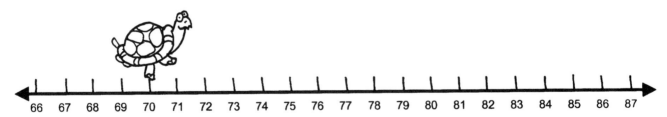

Name

Fill in the missing numbers.

16. Count forward by **1**s.

98 [ ] [ ] [ ] **102**

17. Count backward by **1**s.

253 [ ] **251** **250** [ ]

18. Count forward by **2**s.

86 [ ] [ ] [ ] **94**

19. Count backward by **2**s.

100 [ ] [ ] [ ] [ ]

20. Count forward by **5**s.

[ ] **35** [ ] [ ] **50**

21. Count backward by **5**s.

85 [ ] [ ] [ ] [ ]

22. Count forward by **10**s.

[ ] **90** [ ] [ ] [ ]

23. Count forward by **100**s.

200 [ ] [ ] [ ] [ ]

24. Count backward by **10**s.

[ ] **230** [ ] [ ] [ ]

25. Rocky had **10** packages of juicy bushberry candies. Each package had **5** candies, so he had **50** candies all together. Rocky gave **6** packages to his friend.

Since each package had **5** candies, count backwards from **50** by **5** to find out how many candies Rocky had left.

_____

Name

Reading & Writing Numbers

Name _____   Possible Correct Answers: 25

Date _____   Your Correct Answers: _____

Match the numbers from Roxanne's rock with the word names below.
Write the correct number.

_____ 1. twenty-two

_____ 2. eighty-six

_____ 3. one hundred
three

_____ 4. one half

_____ 5. two hundred
twenty

_____ 6. sixty-seven cents

_____ 7. fourteen

_____ 8. forty

The friends are doing their exercises. Write the number for each problem.

9. Rap does **one hundred forty-two** push-ups.

Write the number. _____

10. Trixie does **seven hundred eighty** leg lifts.

Write the number. _____

11. Fuzzy does **eight hundred sixty-nine** sit-ups.

Write the number. _____

12. Ty does **one thousand, two hundred, fifty-six** tail lifts.

Write the number. _____

13. Which words match the number? *(Circle the letter.)*

790

A. seven hundred nine
B. seven hundred ninety

14. Which words match the number? *(Circle the letter.)*

5,310

A. five hundred thirty-one
B. five thousand, three hundred ten

15. Which words match this number? *(Circle the letter.)*

4,110

A. four thousand one
B. four hundred ten
C. four thousand ten
D. four thousand one hundred
E. four thousand one hundred ten

Name

Second Grade Book of Math Tests

Each friend is bragging about the number of times
he or she has bounced.
Write the number in words.

16. _____

17. _____

18. _____

19. _____

20. _____

21. _____

Name

The swamp animals know some big numbers.

Choose the correct numeral to go with each story. *(Circle the letter.)*

22. Stella and Trixie run laps around their neighborhood every day.
Last year they ran **seventeen thousand** laps.
Which number is this?
    A. 1,700
    B. 17,000
    C. 170,000

23. Terra practices fancy flying swoops every day.
She has done **ninety thousand, nine hundred** different swoops.
Which number is this?
    A. 90,900
    B. 99,000
    C. 9,900
    D. 99,900

24. Rocky picked up **thirty-four thousand** mud balls last year.
Which number is this?
    A. 340,000
    B. 3,400,000
    C. 3,400
    D. 34,000

25. The golf ball factory made **two million** mud balls last year.
Which number is this?
    A. 20,000,000
    B. 2,000,000,000
    C. 2,000,000
    D. 200,000

Name

19

Number Concepts

Name _____

Possible Correct Answers: 30

Date _____

Your Correct Answers: _____

1. What are the **even numbers** on the volcanoes?

   Write them: _____

2. What are the **odd numbers** on the volcanoes?

   Write them: _____

3. Which numeral matches this?
(Circle the letter.)

50 + 6

A. 556

B. 56

C. 506

4. Which numeral matches this?
(Circle the letter.)

900 + 50 + 7

A. 957

B. 900,507

C. 90,507

5. Which numeral matches this?
(Circle the letter.)

4000 + 600 + 3

A. 4,063

B. 463

C. 4,603

6. Which number is in the **tens** place?

384

Answer: _____

7. Which number is in the **hundreds** place?

4,613

Answer: _____

8. Which number is in the **ones** place?

6,285

Answer: _____

9. In this number, in which place is the **3**?
(Circle the letter.)

9,301

A. ones   C. hundreds

B. tens   D. thousands

Name

21

Round these numbers to the nearest ten.

10. **27** _____   14. **31** _____

11. **12** _____   15. **88** _____

12. **79** _____   16. **63** _____

13. **44** _____   17. **55** _____

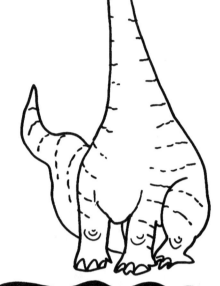

Round these numbers to the nearest hundred.

18. **314** _____   21. **650** _____

19. **525** _____   22. **602** _____

20. **875** _____   23. **255** _____

Name

Second Grade Book of Math Tests   Copyright ©2001 by Incentive Publications, Inc., Nashville, TN.

The Stone Age friends are sky diving with their new parachutes.
The chart tells how long each one floated in the air.
Use the chart to answer questions 24–30.

24. Whose length of time is
    about 50 minutes?

    _____

25. Whose length of time is
    about 100 minutes?

    _____

26. Who stayed in the air almost
    70 minutes?

    _____

27. Whose length of time is
    about 20 minutes?

    _____

28. Who stayed in the air almost
    1000 minutes?

    _____

29. Whose length of time is
    about 150 minutes?

    _____

30. Whose length of time is
    about 300 minutes?

    _____

AIR-TIME CHART
Minutes Floating in the Air

Ty	68
Trixie	289
Roxanne	788
Stella	99
Terra	996
Fuzzy	149
Rocky	48
Brock	18

Name

23

Place Value

Name _____   Possible Correct Answers: 25

Date _____   Your Correct Answers: _____

1. Circle the number with the greatest value in the **tens place**.

840   162   909

18   44

2. Circle the number with the greatest value in the **ones place**.

993   68   3,555

100,000   42

3. Circle the number with the greatest value in the
   hundreds place.

3,014   55,222   594

1,199   482

4. Circle the number with the greatest value in the **thousands place**.

90,000   43,111

8,300   100,002

Write one of these words for each answer:

ones

tens

hundreds

thousands

Look at the number.
Answer questions 5-8 by writing the name of the place value.

68,049

5. The **4** is in the_____ place.

6. The **0** is in the_____ place.

7. The **8** is in the_____ place.

8. The **9** is in the_____ place.

9. Which number has **7** in the **hundreds** place?
   (Circle the letter.)

   A. 5,702

   B. 67,214

   C. 9,876

   D. 4,567

10. Which number has **4** in the **tens** place?
    (Circle the letter.)

    A. 4,123

    B. 404

    C. 8,945

    D. 3,402

11. Circle the stone that has **6** in the **thousands** place.

Name

Second Grade Book of Math Tests

Help Rocky with his math test. Write a number to answer each question.

MATH TEST

12. Write a number with four tens._____

13. Write a number with six hundreds._____

14. Write a number with three ones._____

15. Write a number with two thousands._____

16. Write a 3-digit number with no ones._____

17. Write a 3-digit number with 7 tens._____

18. Write a 4-digit number with 5 hundreds._____

19. Write a 4-digit number with 0 tens._____

20. Write a 3-digit number with 9 tens._____

21. Write a 3-digit number with 8 ones._____

Name

Use Trixie's chart to answer questions 22–25.

22. Which team's score is a number that shows:

   five thousands
   six hundreds
   three tens
   seven ones

Answer: _____

23. Which team's score is a number that shows:

   seven tens
   two ones
   three thousands

Answer: _____

24. Which team's score is a number that shows:

   eight hundreds
   five ones
   six thousands

Answer: _____

25. Which team's score is a number that shows:

   two hundreds
   four ones
   seven tens

Answer: _____

Granite Rock Weight Club

WEIGHT-LIFTING TEAMS

	Team Scores
Granite Lifters	3,702
Tough Guys	274
Bold Boulders	6,805
Stone Giants	8,650
100 Pound Club	3,072
Rock Champs	5,637
Brave Boulders	247
Mighty Muscles	5,367

Name

Second Grade Book of Math Tests

Number Relationships

Name _____   Possible Correct Answers: 25

Date _____   Your Correct Answers: _____

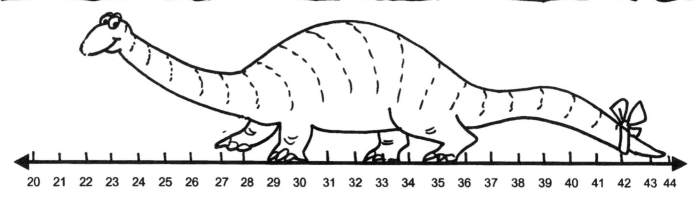

1. Find the number below Ty's nose.

   What can be found at a number that is **20 greater** than the number below Ty's nose? *(Circle the letter.)*

   A. a spot on Ty   B. a bow on his tail   C. a foot

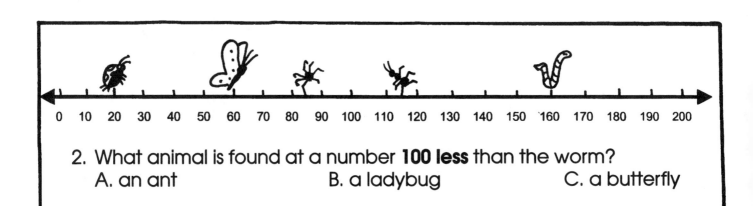

2. What animal is found at a number **100 less** than the worm?

   A. an ant   B. a ladybug   C. a butterfly

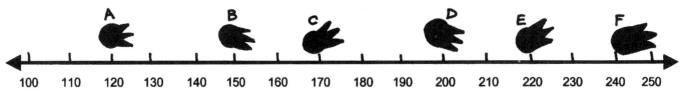

3. Which footprint is at a number **50 greater** than footprint C? _____

28

4. Circle the smallest number.

622   262   622
296
692   66

5. Circle the largest number.

898   888
896   889   89
89   809

Use words to compare the two numbers.
Write **less than** or **greater than** in each blank.

6. **437** is _____ 473

7. $\frac{1}{8}$ is _____ $\frac{1}{2}$

8. **1250** is _____ 1205

9. **660,000** is _____ 6,000

10. **792** is _____ 769

Write <, >, or = in each box.

11. **505** [ ] **500 + 5**

12. **317** [ ] **371**

13. **1,000** [ ] **1,001**

14. **400 + 60** [ ] **406**

Name

Second Grade Book of Math Tests

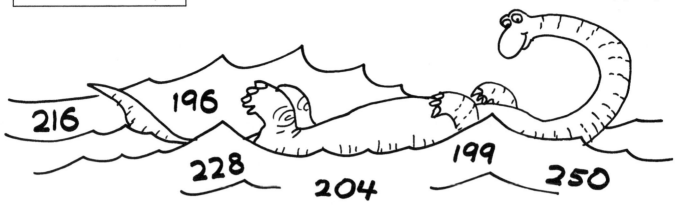

15. Look at the numbers in the waves.

Write the numbers in order from **smallest to largest**.

_____, _____, _____, _____, _____, _____

16.

Granite Burger	$ 4.20
Bushberry Shake	$ 2.40
Grassy Salad	$ 3.05
Sunflower Cake	$ 3.50
Sun Bubble Gum	$ .65

17.

Roxanne	42 pounds
Ty	1,700 pounds
Terra	17 pounds
Stella	970 pounds
Rocky	46 pounds

Put the prices in order from **least to greatest**.

Write them on the lines below.

_____

_____

_____

_____

_____

Put the weights in order from **least to greatest**.

Write them on the lines below.

_____

_____

_____

_____

_____

Name

18. Circle the number that is NOT the same amount as the others.
   A. 2,000 + 200 + 20 + 2
   B. 2,222
   C. two thousand two hundred
   D. 2 thousand, 2 hundred, 22

19. Write a number that is the same as **400 + 30 + 6**.

   _____

20. Write a number that is **10 less than 820**.

   _____

21. Write a number that is $\frac{1}{2}$ **of 100**.

   _____

22. Write a number that is **50 greater than 450**.

   _____

Read the statements below. Draw an **X** on statements that do NOT make sense.

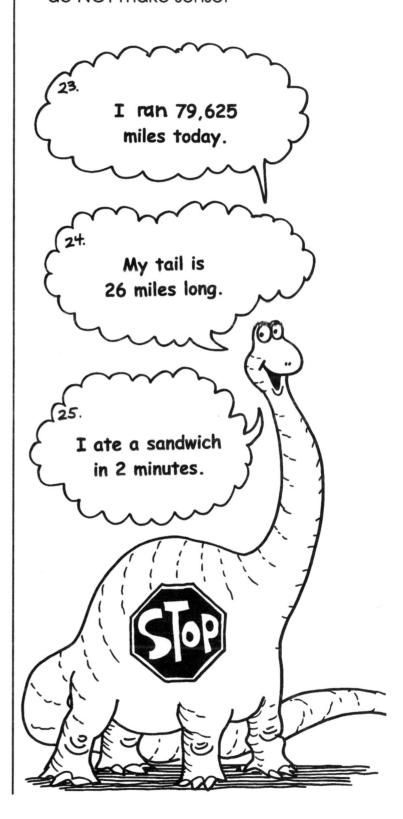

23. I ran 79,625 miles today.

24. My tail is 26 miles long.

25. I ate a sandwich in 2 minutes.

Second Grade Book of Math Tests

Computation Skills Checklists

Computation Test # 1:
ADDITION FACTS
Test Location: pages 34–39

Skill	*Test Items*
Demonstrate knowledge of addition facts with sums to 12	1–15, 21, 22, 25–27
Demonstrate knowledge of addition facts with sums from 13–18	16–20, 23, 24, 28, 31, 32
Use knowledge of addition facts to solve word problems with one-digit addends	16–20, 24
Identify number pairs which have the same sum	25
Recognize and use the commutative property of addition	29, 30
Use knowledge of addition facts to add a column of one-digit addends	31, 32
Identify the numbers in fact families	33, 34
Solve word problems with column addition	35

Computation Test # 2:
ADDITION WITH 2 AND 3 DIGITS
Test Location: pages 40–43

Skill	*Test Items*
Determine accuracy of answers to addition problems	1–3
Solve 2–digit addition problems with no renaming	1, 2, 8–11
Solve 2–digit addition problems with renaming	3, 12, 14
Solve word problems by addition 2–digit numbers	4–7
Solve column addition problems	7, 13
Solve addition problems with 3–digit addends with no renaming	15
Solve addition problems with 3–digits addends with renaming	16
Estimate answers to addition problems	17
Add multiples of 10 and 100	18–20

Computation Test # 3:
SUBTRACTION FACTS
Test Location: pages 44–47

Skill	*Test Items*
Demonstrate knowledge of subtraction facts with addends whose sums are under 12	1–9, 11–15, 27, 30
Demonstrate knowledge of subtraction facts with addends whose sums are 13–20	10, 16–27, 28, 29, 31
Use knowledge of subtraction facts to solve word problems	16–20, 26, 35
Solve a problem with multiple subtractions	20, 32, 35
Fill in missing numbers in addition sentences	21–25, 28–31
Identify the numbers in fact families	27
Solve subtraction problems where 0 is an addend	30
Determine the accuracy of answers to subtraction fact problems	33, 34

Second Grade Book of Math Tests

Computation Test # 4:
SUBTRACTION WITH 2 AND 3 DIGITS
Test Location: pages 48–51

Skill	*Test Items*
Determine accuracy of answers to addition problems	1–3
Solve 2–digit subtraction problems with no renaming	1–3, 5, 8–10, 12, 13, 15
Solve word problems with subtraction	4–7
Solve 2–digit subtraction problems with renaming	4, 6, 7, 11, 14, 16
Solve 3–digit subtraction problems with no renaming	17
Solve 3–digit subtraction problems with renaming	18
Subtract multiples of 10 and 100	19–25
Find missing numbers in subtraction sentences	19–25
Solve subtraction equations	20–25

Computation Test # 5:
ADDITION & SUBTRACTION
Test Location: pages 52–55

Skill	*Test Items*
Find missing numbers in fact families	1–4
Choose the correct operation to solve word problems	5–6
Choose the correct operation for equations	7–12
Use addition and subtraction to solve word problems	13–17, 25
Determine the accuracy of answers to addition and subtraction problems	18–19
Solve multi-step addition and/or subtraction problems	20–25
Solve problems that involve both addition and subtraction	20, 21, 25

Computation Test # 6:
MULTIPLICATION
Test Location: pages 56–59

Skill	*Test Items*
Demonstrate knowledge of multiplication facts with one or more factors from 1–3	1–3, 5, 6, 10, 11, 13, 17, 24, 27
Demonstrate knowledge of multiplication facts with one or more factors from 4–5	2–4, 6–9, 11–17, 24–30
Use multiplication facts to solve word problems	12–17, 24–27
Identify missing numbers in fact families	18–23
Use multiplication facts to solve problems with multiples of 10	28
Find missing numbers in multiplication equations	28–30

Second Grade Book of Math Tests

Addition Facts

Name _____   Possible Correct Answers: 35

Date _____   Your Correct Answers: _____

Stella has finished her addition test. Check her work.
Circle the number of each problem she has solved correctly.

1. $2 + 7 =$ $\boxed{9}$

2. $6 + 5 =$ $\boxed{12}$

3. $\boxed{12} = 3 + 8$

4. $4 + 3 =$ $\boxed{7}$

5. $5 + 5 =$ $\boxed{10}$

6. $\boxed{12} = 7 + 4$

7. $\boxed{10} = 3 + 6$

8. $6 + 4 =$ $\boxed{10}$

9. $5 + 0 =$ $\boxed{0}$

10. $7 + 3 =$ $\boxed{10}$

11. $\boxed{13} = 6 + 6$

12. $9 + 1 =$ $\boxed{11}$

13. $\boxed{8} = 4 + 4$

14. $5 + 4 =$ $\boxed{9}$

15.
$$\begin{array}{r} 7 \\ + 5 \\ \hline \end{array}$$
$\boxed{11}$

16. Rap jumped 6 feet yesterday.

Today he jumped 7 feet farther than yesterday.

How far did Rap jump today?

Answer: _____ feet

18. Roxanne climbed 8 feet today.

Yesterday she climbed 7 feet higher.

How high did she climb yesterday?

Answer: _____ feet

17. Trixie jumped over 9 puddles before lunch.

After lunch, she jumped over 9 more puddles.

How many puddles has Trixie jumped?

Answer: _____ puddles

19. Rocky climbed 7 feet up the rope.

After a rest, he climbed 7 more feet.

How high did Rocky climb?

Answer: _____ feet

Name

35

20. Terra ran 8 miles.

She stopped for a rest.

She ran 5 more miles.

How far did Terra run?

Answer: _____ miles

Find the sums.

21. 3 and 5 are _____

22. 8 and 4 are _____

23. The sum of 5 and 9 is _____

Name

Second Grade Book of Math Tests

Copyright ©2001 by Incentive Publications, Inc., Nashville, TN.

24. Brock has 8 blisters.

Ty has 8 blisters.

Together, they have _____ blisters.

25.

Which number is
the sum for all of these?
Circle the runner
that has the answer.

3 + 8

4 + 7

5 + 6

9 + 2

Name

Second Grade Book of Math Tests

26. **2** plus **6** equals _____.

27. **9** plus **3** equals _____.

28. **6** plus **9** equals _____.

Write the missing numbers.

29. $4 + 3 = \boxed{} + 4$

30. $6 + \boxed{} = 8 + 6$

31. Solve the problem.

$$\begin{array}{r} 2 \\ 5 \\ +8 \\ \hline \end{array}$$

32. Solve the problem.

$$\begin{array}{r} 7 \\ 2 \\ +\ 6 \\ \hline \end{array}$$

Name

38

33. What are the numbers that add up to **12**?

Fill in the missing numbers.

6 + ☐

5 + ☐

☐ + 8

☐ + 4

34. What are the numbers that add up to **13**?

Fill in the missing numbers.

☐ + 9

☐ + 5

6 + ☐

3 + ☐

35. Fuzzy was very thirsty after the race.

He drank 5 glasses of water.

Then he drank 4 glasses of water.

Then he drank 9 more glasses of water.

How much water did Fuzzy drink?

Answer: _____ glasses

Name

39

Addition with 2 and 3 Digits

Name _____   Possible Correct Answers: 20

Date _____   Your Correct Answers: _____

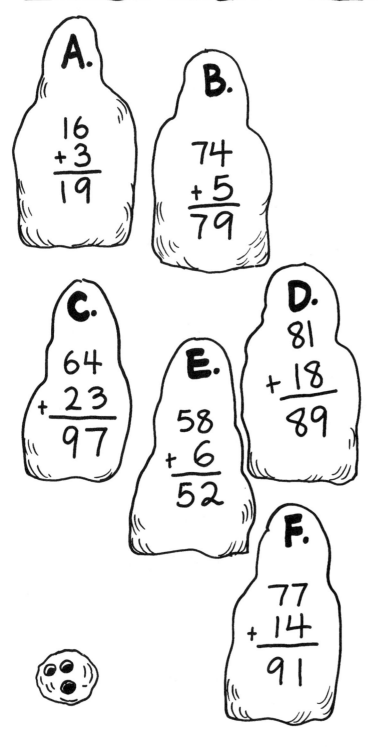

A.

16
+3
19

B.

74
+5
79

C.

64
+23
97

E.

58
+6
52

D.

81
+18
89

F.

77
+14
91

1. Look at problems A and B. Which problems are correct?

   Circle one of these answers.

   Problem A   Problem B

   Both problems   Neither problem

2. Look at problems C and D. Which problems are correct?

   Circle one of these answers.

   Problem C   Problem D

   Both problems   Neither problem

3. Look at problems E and F. Which problems are correct?

   Circle one of these answers.

   Problem E   Problem F

   Both problems   Neither problem

Second Grade Book of Math Tests   Copyright ©2001 by Incentive Publications, Inc., Nashville, TN.

ROCK BOWLING SCORES
(Number of Pins Knocked Down)

Fuzzy	46
Rocky	29
Stella	13
Brock	88
Rap	50
Trixie	32
Roxanne	61

4. Rap knocked down _____ pins.

   Trixie knocked down _____ pins.

   Together they knocked down

   A. 18 pins.

   B. 82 pins.

   C. 80 pins.

5. Fuzzy knocked down _____ pins.

   Rocky knocked down _____ pins.

   Together they knocked down

   A. 75 pins.
   B. 23 pins.
   C. 65 pins.

6. Roxanne scored _____ .

   Stella scored _____ .

   The total of their scores

   is _____ .

7. Rocky scored _____ .

   Trixie scored _____ .

   Brock scored _____ .

   The total of their scores is _____ .

Name

Second Grade Book of Math Tests

8. Ten more than 45 is _____.

9. Five more than 11 is _____.

10. Six more than 53 is _____.

11. Three more than 60 is _____.

12. Eight more than 22 is _____.

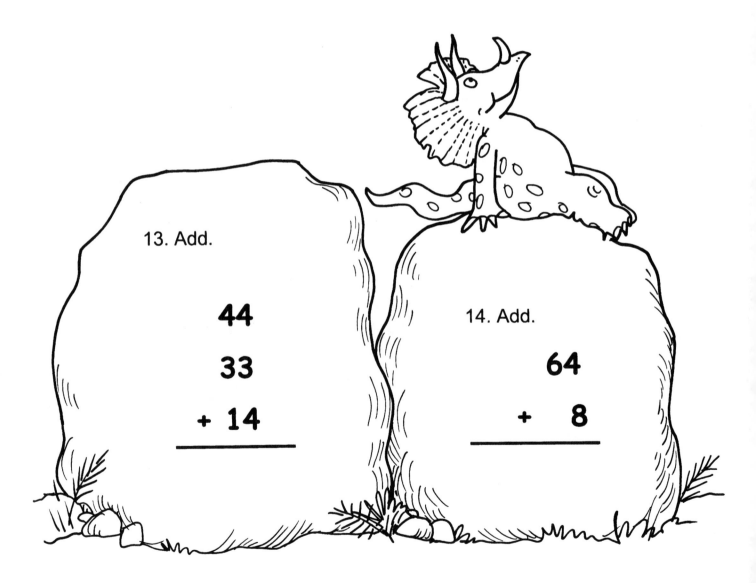

13. Add.

$$\begin{array}{r} 44 \\ 33 \\ + 14 \\ \hline \end{array}$$

14. Add.

$$\begin{array}{r} 64 \\ + 8 \\ \hline \end{array}$$

Name

42

15.

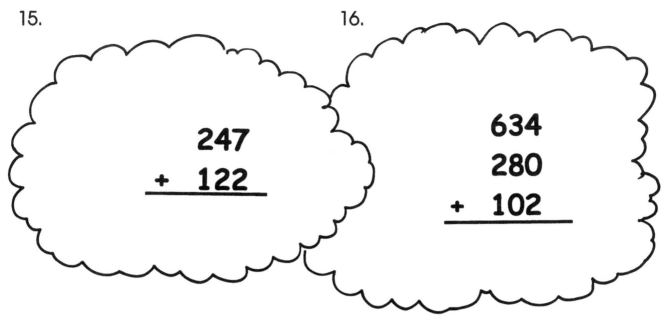

$$
\begin{array}{r}
247 \\
+ 122 \\
\hline
\end{array}
$$

16.

$$
\begin{array}{r}
634 \\
280 \\
+ 102 \\
\hline
\end{array}
$$

17. **22 + 57** is closest to:

A. 50   B. 60   C. 70   D. 80   E. 90

Fill in the missing numbers.

18. **30** + ☐ = **90**

19. ☐ + **10** = **50**

20. **200** + ☐ = **700**

Name

Second Grade Book of Math Tests

Subtraction Facts

Name _____

Date _____

Possible Correct Answers: 35

Your Correct Answers: _____

Rocky has finished his addition and subtraction test. Check his work.
Circle the number of each problem that he has answered correctly.

1. **12 - 3 =** $\boxed{8}$

2. **9 -** $\boxed{11}$ **= 2**

3. **8 =** $\boxed{12}$ **+ 4**

4. **11 - 4 =** $\boxed{7}$

5. **6 +** $\boxed{6}$ **= 12**

6. **8 - 5 =** $\boxed{3}$

7. $\boxed{4}$ **= 11 - 8**

8. **10 -** $\boxed{3}$ **= 7**

9. $\boxed{8}$ **- 2 = 6**

10. **13 - 3 =** $\boxed{16}$

11. **3 +** $\boxed{3}$ **= 6**

12. **9 - 4 =** $\boxed{5}$

13. $\boxed{5}$ **+ 5 = 11**

14. **12 - 5 =** $\boxed{7}$

15. **8**
   + $\boxed{0}$
   _____
   10

16. Stella started the game with 18 marbles.

    She lost 9 marbles during the game.

    How many marbles were left?

    Answer: _____

17. Trixie had 15 marbles.

    She lost 8 marbles.

    How many marbles were left?

    Answer: _____

18. Fuzzy had 14 new marbles.

    He gave away 6 marbles.

    How many marbles did he have left?

    Answer: _____

19. Trixie had 17 marbles.

    8 were green.

    The rest were red.

    How many marbles were red?

    Answer: _____

20. A player started a marbles game with 17 marbles.

    She lost 8 marbles in the game.

    Then she gave away 3 marbles.

    How many marbles were left?

    Answer: _____

Name

45

21. Six and _____ are 15.

22. _____ and seven are 14.

23. Eight and _____ are 12.

24. Nine and _____ are 16.

25. Seven and _____ are 11.

26. Rocky had 14 pieces of chalk.

   He used 9 of them to draw his hopscotch.

   How many pieces did he have left?

   Answer: _____

27. The same number is missing from all of the number sentences below.

   The missing number is one of the numbers on the hopscotch grid.

   Fill in the missing number.

   11 − ☐ = 4

   12 − 5 = ☐

   ☐ − 5 = 2

   13 − 6 = ☐

Name

Second Grade Book of Math Tests   Copyright ©2001 by Incentive Publications, Inc., Nashville, TN.

28. 16 minus 8 =_____

29. 19 minus _____ = 9

30. _____ minus 10 = 0

31. 20 minus _____ = 20

32. Subtract.

18 – 9 – 4 = ____

33. Which is correct?
Circle the letter.

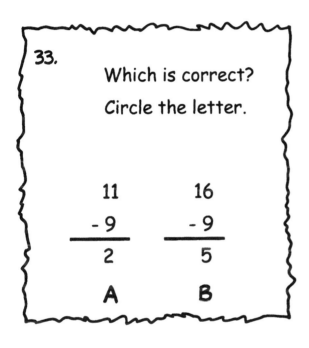

11	16
- 9	- 9
2	5
A	**B**

34. Which is correct?
Circle the letter.

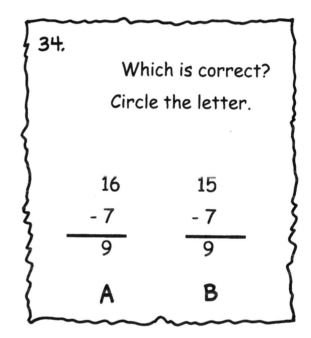

16	15
- 7	- 7
9	9
A	**B**

35. Fuzzy started at 0 on the number line.   Then he stopped.
He hopped 20 spaces forward.   Where did he stop? _____
Then he hopped backward 9 spaces.
Then he hopped forward 4 spaces.

Name

Second Grade Book of Math Tests

Subtraction with 2 and 3 Digits

Name _____

Possible Correct Answers: 25

Date _____

Your Correct Answers: _____

1. Look at Problem A and Problem B.

   Which answer is correct? *(Circle the answer.)*

   Problem A   Problem B   Both answers   Neither answer

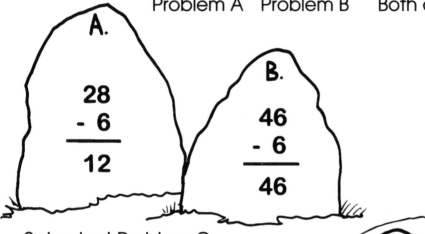

A.
$$28$$
$$- 6$$
$$12$$

B.
$$46$$
$$- 6$$
$$46$$

2. Look at Problem C
   and Problem D.

   Which answer is correct?
   (Circle the answer.)

   Problem C
   Problem D
   Both answers
   Neither answer

C.
$$59$$
$$- 23$$
$$36$$

D.
$$88$$
$$- 77$$
$$11$$

E.
$$67$$
$$- 55$$
$$12$$

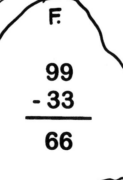

F.
$$99$$
$$- 33$$
$$66$$

3. Look at Problem E
   and Problem F.

   Which answer is correct?
   (Circle the answer.)

   Problem E
   Problem E
   Both answers
   Neither answer

Second Grade Book of Math Tests

Copyright ©2001 by Incentive Publications, Inc., Nashville, TN.

NEW SKATES

Fuzzy	☐
Rocky	$ 59
Rap	☐
Stella	$ 28
Trixie	$ 72
Roxanne	☐
Brock	$ 43
Terra	☐

Use the chart to find skate prices.

4. Brock's skates cost _____.

   Rap's skates cost $17 less.

   What is the cost of Rap's skates?

   A. $ 36

   B. $ 60

   C. $ 26

5. Rocky's skates cost _____ .

   Fuzzy's skates cost $26 less.

   What is the cost of
   Fuzzy's skates?

   Answer: _____

6. Trixie's skates cost _____ .

   Roxanne's skates
   cost $36 less.

   What is the cost of
   Roxanne's skates?

   Answer: _____

7. Together, Terra's skates
   and Stella's skates cost $46.

   What is the cost of
   Terra's skates?

   Answer: _____

Name

Second Grade Book of Math Tests

8. Ten less than 66 is _____ .

9. Five less than 35 is _____ .

10. 48 is eight more than _____ .

11. Seven less than 100 is _____ .

12. Eighteen less than 18 is _____ .

13. Three less than 73 is _____ .

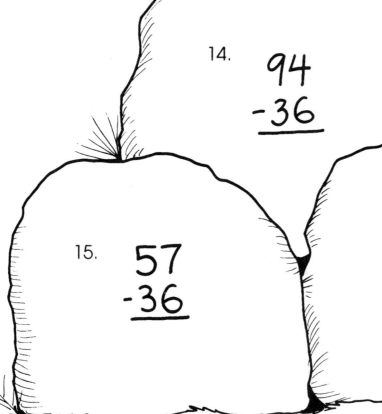

14.
$$\begin{array}{r} 94 \\ -36 \\ \hline \end{array}$$

15.
$$\begin{array}{r} 57 \\ -36 \\ \hline \end{array}$$

16.
$$\begin{array}{r} 83 \\ -58 \\ \hline \end{array}$$

Name _____

Second Grade Book of Math Tests

17. Circle the correct answer.

$$695$$
$$- 265$$

A. 430   B. 435

18. Circle the correct answer.

$$708$$
$$- 319$$

A. 389   B. 491

19. 160 skates – ☐ skates = 100 skates

20. 150 skaters – 80 skaters = ☐ skaters

21. Twenty minus twenty is ☐ .

22. Eighty minus 30 is ☐ .

23. $900 – $600 = $☐

24. 140 – 50 = ☐

25. 100 – ☐ = 70

Name

Second Grade Book of Math Tests

Addition & Subtraction

Name _____

Possible Correct Answers: 25

Date _____

Your Correct Answers: _____

1.

$11 - 8 = \boxed{}$

$3 + \boxed{} = 11$

$8 + 3 = \boxed{}$

$\boxed{} - 3 = 8$

2.

$\boxed{} + 7 = 15$

$15 - \boxed{} = 7$

$8 + \boxed{} = 15$

$15 - \boxed{} = 8$

3.

$17 - 8 = \boxed{}$

$9 + \boxed{} = 17$

$17 - \boxed{} = 9$

$\boxed{} + 8 = 17$

4.

$12 - 3 = \boxed{}$

$3 + \boxed{} = 12$

$9 + 3 = \boxed{}$

$\boxed{} - 9 = 3$

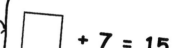

5. How should you solve the problem?

Read the problem. Choose one answer.

Rap danced 68 hours this week.

Stella danced 14 hours less.

How many hours did Stella dance?

To solve this problem, you should...

A. Add   B. Subtract

6. How should you solve the problem below?
Read the problem. Choose one answer.

Roxanne has 17 blisters from dancing.

Stella has 14 blisters.

Rap has 36 blisters.

All together, how many blisters do the friends have?

To solve this problem, you should...

A. Add   B. Subtract

Write **+** or **–** in each box.

7. **28** ☐ **30 = 58**

8. **32** ☐ **12 = 20**

9. **66** ☐ **6 = 60**

10. **7** ☐ **9 = 8** ☐ **8**

11. **500** ☐ **150 = 650**

12. **25** ☐ **5** ☐ **5 = 35**

Name

Second Grade Book of Math Tests

13. The longest dance line had 118 dancers.
The shortest line had 50 dancers.
What is the difference between the two lines?

      A. 168 dancers

      B. 58 dancers

      C. 68 dancers

      D. none of these answers

14. Trixie's dance team drank 34 quarts of water.

Ty's dance team drank 17 quarts of water.

How much water did they drink all together?

Answer: _____

16. 385 fans watched the Rock Rhumba Dance.

261 fans watched the Stone City Salsa Dance.

How many more fans watched the rhumba?

Answer: _____

15. Rocky and Roxanne learned 28 dances.

Rap and Terra learned 46 dances.

How many more did Rap and Terra learn?

Answer: _____

DANCE CONTEST
Tickets Sold

Friday	260 tickets
Saturday	153 tickets
Sunday	218 tickets

17. How many tickets were sold in the three days? _____

Name

18. Is the answer correct?

Circle **yes** or **no**.

19. Is the answer correct?

Circle **yes** or **no**.

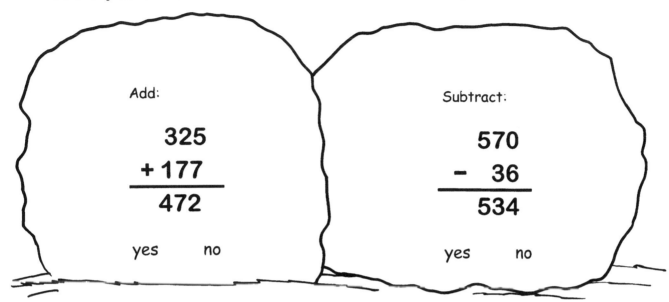

Add:

$$\begin{array}{r} 325 \\ + 177 \\ \hline 472 \end{array}$$

yes   no

Subtract:

$$\begin{array}{r} 570 \\ - 36 \\ \hline 534 \end{array}$$

yes   no

Fill in the missing numbers.

20. **7 + 20 – 10 =** ☐

21. **8 + 8 – 3 =** ☐

22. **50 – 20 – 10 =** ☐

23. **19 – 9 – 10 =** ☐

24. **100 + 500 + 20 =** ☐

25. Rocky and Roxanne won 25 + 5 trophies.

Rap and Terra won 40 – 15 trophies.

Who won more? _____

Name

Second Grade Book of Math Tests

Multiplication

Name _____   Possible Correct Answers: 30

Date _____   Your Correct Answers: _____

1. Look at the 3 scooters.

   There are 2 wheels on each scooter.

   How many wheels all together?

   Answer: _____

2. 3 fives is _____	7. 6 fives is _____
3. 7 twos is _____	8. 0 fours is _____
4. 4 fours is _____	9. 10 fives is _____
5. 3 threes is _____	10. 3 twos is _____
6. 2 sixes is _____	11. 2 sevens is _____

Second Grade Book of Math Tests

12. Trixie did 6 practice jumps each day. She practiced 5 days.
How many jumps did she try?

Answer: _____

13. Trixie took 8 falls during each hour that she rode her skateboard.
She rode her skateboard 3 hours.
How many times did she fall?

Answer: _____

14. Trixie has 7 bruises on her right front leg.
She has 7 bruises on her left front leg.
She has 7 bruises on her right rear leg.
She has no bruises on her left rear leg.
How many bruises does she have?

Answer: _____

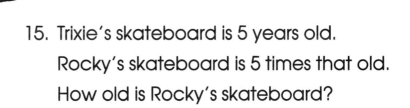

15. Trixie's skateboard is 5 years old.
Rocky's skateboard is 5 times that old.
How old is Rocky's skateboard?

Answer: _____ years old

Name

57

16. Four friends each have four legs.
How many legs all together?

_____

17. Trixie took six rides on her skateboard.
She did two flips during each ride.
How many flips all together?

_____

Write the missing numbers.

18. **4 x 6 = ☐ x 4**

21. **6 x ☐ = 3 x 6**

19. **5 x ☐ = 3 x 5**

22. **4 x ☐ = 5 x 4**

20. **☐ x 7 = 7 x 2**

23. **☐ x 9 = 9 x 3**

Ooops!

Name _____

Cold Drinks
Gooey Green Juice 9 ¢
Fizzy Root Beer 7 ¢
Rainwater Slush 5 ¢
Moss Shake 10 ¢

Multiply to find the costs below.

24. 3 fizzy root beers: _____

25. 8 moss shakes: _____

26. 4 rainwater slush drinks: _____

27. 2 gooey green juice drinks: _____

28. Circle the problem with the correct answer.

A. **50 x 3 = 150**   B. **3 x 90 = 210**

29. Circle the problem with the correct answer.

A. **8 x 3 = 24**   B. **5 x 6 = 35**

30. Circle the problem with the correct answer.

A. **7 x 4 = 24**   B. **2 x 9 = 18**

Name

Second Grade Book of Math Tests

Fractions & Money Skills Checklists

Fractions & Money Test # 1:

FRACTIONS

Test Location: pages 62–65

Skill	*Test Items*
Name fractional parts of a set	1–4
Read and write fractions	5–10, 23, 24, 28, 29
Name fractional parts of a whole	11–18
Identify fractional parts of a dollar	19–22
Read and write mixed numerals	25–27
Solve word problems with fractions	30
Recognize fractional parts of an hour	30

Second Grade Book of Math Tests

Fractions & Money Test # 2:

MONEY

Test Location: pages 66–69

Skill	*Test Items*
Recognize the amount of money represented by coins that are pictured	1, 2, 5, 13, 20
Recognize the amount of money represented by coins that are not pictured	3–4
Identify coins that comprise an amount of money	6–8
Recognize that an amount of money can be made with different groupings of coins and/or dollars	7, 8
Solve word problems with money	8–12, 20
Add and subtract amounts of money	9–12, 17–19
Estimate answers to problems with money	12
Use symbols to compare amounts of money	13–16

Fractions

Name _____   Possible Correct Answers: 30

Date _____   Your Correct Answers: _____

Rap has nine eggs
in his basket.

1. What fraction
   has stripes?_____

2. What fraction
   has dots? _____

3. What fraction
   are black? _____

4. What fraction
   has a crack? _____

Write a fraction for each.

5. one half _____

6. two thirds _____

7. one fourth _____

8. four sixths _____

9. two fifths _____

10. six tenths _____

Look at the shapes.

Write the letter of the shapes that match each of these descriptions:

A.

B.

11. $\frac{1}{2}$ is colored black _____

12. $\frac{2}{3}$ have flowers _____

C.

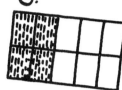

13. $\frac{1}{4}$ is white _____

D.

14. $\frac{4}{10}$ have lines _____

E.

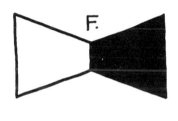

F.

G.

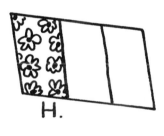

H.

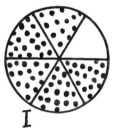

I.

J.

Write a fraction for each answer.

15. What part of shape H has flowers? _____

K.

16. What part of shape J is plain white? _____

L.

17. What part of shape I has spots? _____

18. What part of shape M has NO spots? _____

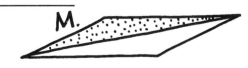

M.

Name

63

19. Roxanne wins $\frac{1}{2}$ of a dollar for each trick she does well.

    Which set of coins shows that amount of money?

    Circle one letter.

 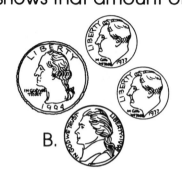 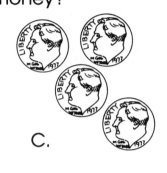

A.   B.   C.

20. Roxanne wants to give $\frac{1}{4}$ of a dollar to her friend Rocky.

    Circle the coins that she could use.

21. Stella's new jumping shoes cost $\frac{3}{4}$ of a dollar.

    Which answer equals that amount of money?
    A. 2 quarters and 5 nickels
    B. 2 quarters and 6 nickels
    C. 6 dimes and 10 pennies
    D. 12 nickels

22. Fuzzy earned $\frac{1}{10}$ of a dollar for his new trick.

    Which answer equals that amount?
    A. 10 dimes
    B. 5 dimes
    C. 6 nickels
    D. 1 nickel and 5 pennies

Fuzzy Tricks

Name

Match the numerals to the words.
For each problem, write the fraction or mixed numeral from the list.

23. one sixth _____

24. six eighths _____

25. one and one sixth _____

26. five and two thirds _____

27. six and two tenths _____

28. three fifths _____

29. three sixths _____

$5\frac{2}{3}$

$\frac{1}{6}$

$6\frac{2}{10}$

$\frac{3}{5}$

$\frac{6}{8}$

$1\frac{1}{6}$

$\frac{3}{6}$

30. Stella stood on her head for $\frac{1}{2}$ hour.

Ty stood on his head for $\frac{3}{4}$ of an hour.

Brock stood on his head for $\frac{1}{4}$ of an hour.

Who did this trick the longest?

Answer: _____

Name

Second Grade Book of Math Tests

Money

Name _____

Possible Correct Answers: 20

Date _____

Your Correct Answers: _____

1. Roxanne has this much money for snacks at the mudball game.

How much does she have?

_____ ¢

2. Stella has this much money for snacks at the game.

How much does she have?

_____ ¢

3. Fuzzy has:

3 dimes

2 nickels

3 pennies

How much? _____ ¢

4. Rap has:

1 quarter

4 dimes

7 pennies

How much? _____ ¢

5. Which amount of money is more? Circle it.

A.

B.

6. Which makes **70¢** ?

Circle one answer.
 A. 2 quarters & 2 nickels
 B. 6 dimes & 2 nickels
 C. 10 pennies & 2 quarters
 D. 8 nickels & 2 dimes

7. Which does NOT makes **55¢** ?
Circle one answer.
 A. 5 dimes and 5 pennies
 B. 11 nickels
 C. 1 quarter and 4 dimes
 D. 1 quarter, 2 dimes,
    and 2 nickels

8. Rocky has 10 dimes.
 Rap has 20 nickels.
 Brock has 3 quarters and
    4 nickels.
 Stella has 8 dimes and
    20 pennies.
 Who does NOT have **$1.00**?

 Answer: _____

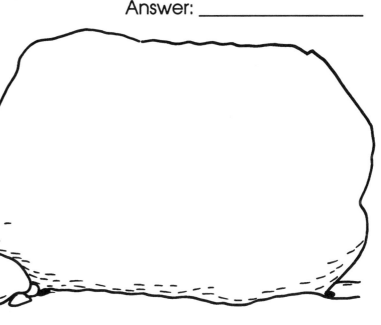

Name

Second Grade Book of Math Tests

SNACKS

Sweet Twig Cookie	25¢ each
Rocky Top Shake	98¢ each
Very Berry Pancakes	$ 1.00 each
Roasted Nut Sticks	5 for 20¢
Spicy Weed Cake	75¢ each
Rock Candy	13¢ each
Tree-Top Gum	4¢ each

SNACK CAVE

9. Roxanne wants a shake, pancakes, and a spicy weed cake. How much will this cost?

   Answer: _____

11. Stella had 95¢. She bought a piece of rock candy and a cookie. How much money did she have left?

    Answer: _____

10. Brock bought 10 nut sticks. How much did this cost?

    Answer: _____

12. Ty wants to buy a shake, pancakes, 1 piece of rock candy, and 5 pieces of gum.

    About how much will this cost?

    A. about $1.30

    B. about $ 2.30

    C. about $ 3.30

    D. about $1.00

Name

For problems 13–16, write <, >, or = in each box.

13.

14. A dollar bill and 3 dimes 6 quarters

15. 78¢  8 dimes

16. 3 quarters and 9 pennies 10 nickels and 3 dimes

17. Add.

$ 1.78
+ $ 5.22
$.

18. Subtract.

$ 8.92
– $ 8.75
$.

19. Multiply.

9¢
x 5¢
¢

20. Roxanne has this much money.

Can she buy the bat?
(Circle yes or no.)

yes   **no**

MUD
BALL
BAT

68¢

Name

69

Second Grade Book of Math Tests

Problem-Solving Skills Checklists

Problem-Solving Test # 1:
PROBLEM SOLVING STRATEGIES
Test Location: pages 72–75

Skill	*Test Items*
Identify or define a problem	1–2
Describe information that is missing from a problem	3
Identify information unnecessary for problem solution	4
Identify operations needed for problem solution	5–7
Translate a problem into an equation	8
Extend a pattern to solve a problem	9
Estimate problem solutions	10–11
Use logic to solve a problem	12
Use mental math to solve a problem	13–14
Select an appropriate strategy for solving a given problem	15

Problem-Solving Test # 2:
PATTERNS
Test Location: pages 76–77

Skill	*Test Items*
Identify a pictured pattern and extend the pattern	1–8, 12
Identify a number sequence and extend the sequence	9–11
Identify a number pattern and extend the pattern	13–15
Use patterns to solve problems	13–15

Second Grade Book of Math Tests   Copyright ©2001 by Incentive Publications, Inc., Nashville, TN.

Problem-Solving Test # 3:
PROBLEMS TO SOLVE
Test Location: pages 80–85

Skill	Test Items
Identify and use an equation to solve a problem	1
Solve a variety of word problems	1–12, 17–30
Solve problems with whole numbers	2, 3, 21
Solve problems using information from charts and tables	4–6, 8, 9
Solve problems with fractions	7
Solve problems involving money	8–9, 28
Solve problems involving time	10–12, 17–18
Use a diagram or illustration to assist with problem solution	13–16, 25–26
Solve problems involving measurements	19, 27, 29, 30
Use mental math to solve a problem	20
Solve problems using information from a graph	22–24
Use logic to solve a problem	25–26
Determine perimeter to solve a problem	29

Problem-Solving Test # 4:
ALGEBRA CONCEPTS
Test Location: pages 86–87

Skill	Test Items
Write or choose an expression to represent a statement	1–2
Recognize meanings of expressions	3–4
Choose an equation to represent a problem	5
Use symbols or words to describe the relationship between numbers	6–8
Solve equations to find a variable	9–10

Problem-Solving Test # 5:
PROBLEM-SOLVING PROCESS
Test Location: pages 88–91

Skill	Test Items
The problem-solving process test is a test of problem-solving performance. A scoring guide (page 140) is used to enable the adult to give students a score of 1–5 in the areas of Understanding, Strategies & Processes, Communication, and Correctness of the answer.	Entire Test

Second Grade Book of Math Tests　　　Copyright ©2001 by Incentive Publications, Inc., Nashville, TN.

Problem-Solving Strategies

Name _____   Possible Correct Answers: 15

Date _____   Your Correct Answers: _____

1. Is this a problem that can be solved? Circle: **yes** or **no**.

   15 swimmers came to the race on Monday.

   Many more came on Tuesday.

   How many swimmers came on Tuesday?

2. Is this a problem that can be solved? Circle: **yes** or **no**.

   20 swimmers finished the race.

   Each swimmer used 5 towels to dry off.

   How many towels were used?

3. What is missing from this problem? (Circle one answer below.)

   Roxanne finished at 1:15 to win first place.

   Rocky won second place.

   How much faster was Roxanne than Rocky?

   A. The time Roxanne finished

   B. The time Rocky finished

   C. The time the race started

4. Read the problem.
   Cross out the sentence that is not needed to solve the problem.

   A swimmer entered 26 races.

   She won 18 races.

   596 fans watched the swimming races.

   How many races did she enter that she did NOT win?

5. To solve problem number 4, you should . . .

   A. Add   B. Subtract   C. Multiply   D. None of these

6. Read the problem.

   Roxanne practiced swimming
   for 5 days.

   She swam 7 miles each day.

   How many miles did
   she swim?

   To solve this problem,
   you should...
   A. Add
   B. Subtract
   C. Multiply
   D. None of these

7. Read the problem.

   Rocky took 22 dives without
   bumping his head.

   He bumped his head on 14 dives.

   How many dives did he take
   all together?

   A. Add
   B. Subtract
   C. Multiply
   D. None of these

Name

73

8. Read the problem and circle the letter of the number sentence that would help to solve the problem.

> Roxanne dove 15 feet below the water.
> Rocky dove 7 feet deeper than Roxanne.
> How deep was Rocky's dive?

A. 15 − 7 = ☐

B. 15 × 7 = ☐

C. 15 + 7 = ☐

9. Find the pattern on this chart. Use the pattern to help solve the problem.

ROCKY'S SWIM PRACTICE

Week # 1 — 2 hours
Week # 2 — 4 hours
Week # 3 — 8 hours
Week # 4 — ☐ hours

How many hours did Rocky practice in Week # 4? _____

10. Estimate the answer.

Rocky saw 792 fish.

Roxanne saw 311 fish.

About how many more fish did Rocky see than Roxanne?

A. about 500 fish

B. about 400 fish

C. about 300 fish

11. Estimate the answer.

Rocky swam . . .

407 meters on Monday.

385 meters on Tuesday.

102 meters on Wednesday.

About how many meters did he swim in those 3 days?

A. about 800 meters

B. about 500 meters

C. about 900 meters

Name

12. Three swimmers entered a race.

Dino finished ahead of Al.

Charlie finished last.

Who won the race? _____

13. The sum of Ty's age and Brock's age is 15 years.

A. If Ty is 8, how old is Brock?

_____

B. If Ty is 6, how old is Brock?

_____

14. Stella is older than Trixie.

The difference between their ages is 5 years.

A. If Trixie is 20, how old is Stella?

_____

B. If Stella is 18, how old is Trixie?

_____

15. Read the problem.

Four friends get together.

Bella is taller than Al. Al is shorter than Charlie.

Dino is taller than Charlie. Bella is taller than Dino.

Who is the tallest?

The best way to solve this problem is . . .

A. Write a number sentence.

B. Estimate the answer.

C. Put numbers on a chart.

D. Draw a picture.

Name

Second Grade Book of Math Tests

Patterns

Name _____   Possible Correct Answers: 15

Date _____   Your Correct Answers: _____

1. Color the last fish in a way that continues the pattern.

2. Color the last shape in a way that continues the pattern.

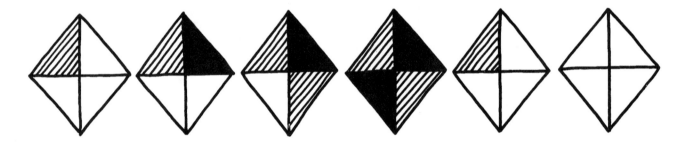

3. Color the last shape in a way that continues the pattern.

 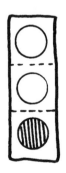   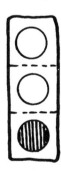 

Second Grade Book of Math Tests   Copyright ©2001 by Incentive Publications, Inc., Nashville, TN.

4. Color the last shape in a way that continues the pattern.

  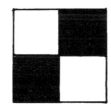  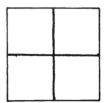

5. Draw the next shape to continue the pattern.

  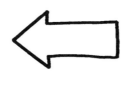 _____

6. Draw the next arrow to continue the pattern.

  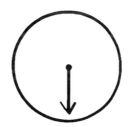 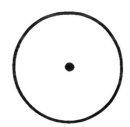

7. Draw the next shape or group of shapes to continue the pattern.

Name

Second Grade Book of Math Tests

8. Rocky is stringing stone beads in a pattern.
   Draw the next four beads he will put on the string.

9. Fill in the missing numbers to continue the pattern.

   2   4   6   8   ☐   ☐   ☐

10. Fill in the missing numbers to continue the pattern.

   100   90   80   ☐   **60**   ☐   ☐   ☐

11. Fill in the missing numbers to continue the pattern.

   2   3   5   8   12   ☐   ☐

12. Roxanne is stringing stone beads in a pattern.
    Draw the next four beads she will put on the string.

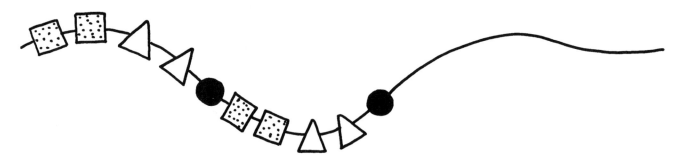

Name

13. Follow the pattern.

Fill in the missing number on Ty's chart.

14. Follow the pattern.

Fill in the missing number on Rap's chart.

15. Follow the pattern.

Fill in the missing number on Brock's chart.

13.

Fish Caught by Ty

Day # 1	1
Day # 2	2
Day # 3	4
Day # 4	7
Day # 5	11
Day # 6	☐

14.

Fish Caught by Rap

Day # 1	32
Day # 2	28
Day # 3	24
Day # 4	20
Day # 5	☐
Day # 6	12

15.

Fish Caught by Brock

Day # 1	2
Day # 2	4
Day # 3	3
Day # 4	6
Day # 5	4
Day # 6	☐

STOP

Name

79

Problems to Solve

Name _____ Possible Correct Answers: 30

Date _____ Your Correct Answers: _____

1. Read the problem.

     240 visitors came to watch the river race.

     The visitors either watched the race from trees or from the river bank.

     Most of them watched the race from the river bank.

     40 sat in trees to watch the race.

     How many visitors watched from the river bank?

Choose the number sentence that will solve the problem.

Use that number sentence to find the answer.

Write the answer in the correct box.

A. **240 + 40 =** ☐

B. **240 – 40 =** ☐

C. **40 – 240 =** ☐

2. Stella's log boat tipped over 8 times during the race.

   Ty's boat tipped over 4 times as many as Stella's.

   How many times did Ty's boat tip?

   Answer: _____

3. Rocky finished the race in 134 minutes.

   It took Terra 37 minutes less to finish.

   How long did Terra take?

   Answer: _____

RIVER-HOPPING CONTEST		
Hopper's Name	Number of Hops to Cross the River	Number of Hops to Return
Brock	14	15
Rap	12	8
Terra	14	11
Trixie	20	24

In the river-hopping contest, four animals hopped across the river and back again. The table shows the number of hops it took to cross the river each way.

4. How many more hops did Terra take crossing the river than returning?

   _____

5. How many hops did Brock need to cross both ways?

   _____

6. Who hopped 3 times as many hops as Rap on the return part of the contest?

   _____

7. After the contest, Rocky ate $\frac{1}{3}$ of a pizza. Roxanne ate $\frac{1}{3}$ of a pizza. Between the two of them, how much pizza did they eat?

   A. $\frac{1}{2}$ of a pizza   B. $\frac{2}{3}$ of a pizza   C. a whole pizza

Use the snack chart for problems 8 and 9.

SNACKS

Crunchie Munchies	15¢
Rock Candy	12¢
Energy Drink	36¢
Stone-Cooked Pizza	50¢

8. Brock and Ty shared a bag of rock candy. Each friend paid for half of the cost. How much did they each pay?

   _____

9. Stella bought crunchie munchies, a pizza, and an energy drink. How much did she pay?

   _____

Name

Rap is looking
at the clock.

10. The diving contest began
2 hours ago.

What time was that?

_____

11. Rap arrived $\frac{1}{2}$ hour ago.

What time was that?

_____

12. The contest will end in $1\frac{1}{2}$
hours from the time shown.

What time will it end?

_____

Use the shape diagram for questions 13–15.

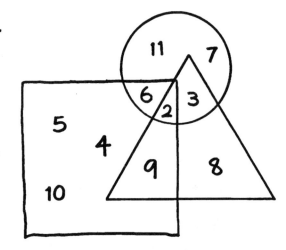

13. What numbers are inside the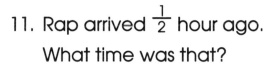

but not in the △ ? _____

14. What numbers are inside both

 the ◯ and the □ ? _____

15. What numbers are outside the △ ? _____

16. What number falls inside all three shapes? _____

17. A diving practice was held
8 days before April 13.

What was the date? _____

18. A diving contest will begin
2 weeks and 3 days from April 5.

On what date will
the contest begin? _____

APRIL

S	M	T	W	Th	F	S
	1	2	3	4	5	6
7	8	9	10	11	12	13
14	15	16	17	18	19	20
21	22	23	24	25	26	27
28	29	30				

19. Stella jumped off a large rock into the pond.
She made a splash that went 18 feet into the air.

Brock jumped off the same rock.
His splash was 24 feet higher than Stella's.

How high was the splash made by Brock? _____

20. 15 sailors raced their boats.

The boats were numbered
from 1 to 15.

In those 15 numbers,
how many times does
the digit 1 (one) appear?

Answer: _____

21. A swimmer swam 28 miles
in one week. The next
week, she swam 18 miles.
How far did she swim in
two weeks?

Answer: _____

Name

Second Grade Book of Math Tests

NUMBER of PEOPLE Fitting on RAFTS	
Rocky's Raft	
Roxanne's Raft	
Freddy's Raft	
Ozzie's Raft	

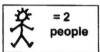 = 2 people

Use the graph for problems 22–24.

22. How many more people can fit on Freddy's raft than on Rocky's?

_____

23. How many people (total) can fit on Roxanne's and Ozzie's rafts?

_____

24. How many fewer people does Ozzie's raft hold than Rocky's?

_____

Use this picture
for problems 25 and 26.

Four swimmers finished the race.

The winner did not wear flippers.

The winner did not have goggles.

The swimmer who finished last was not Fuzzy.

The swimmer who finished last wore goggles.

25. Who won the race?

_____

26. Who finished last?

_____

Name _____

84

27. Terra floated 87 meters on the river.

Rap floated 13 meters further than Terra.

Brock floated twice as far as Rap.

How far did Brock float?

Answer: _____

28. The swimmers spent $ 9.45 on snacks.

The visitors watching the swim race spent $14.35 on snacks.

How much money was spent all together?

Answer: _____

29. Ty rowed around the outside edge of this pond twice.

How far did he row?

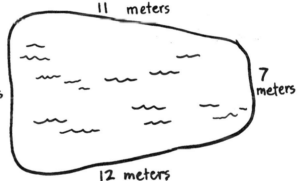

Answer: _____

30. In the race, Ty rowed 565 meters.

Trixie rowed 195 fewer meters than Ty.

How far did Trixie row?

Answer: _____

Name

85

Algebra Concepts

Name _____   Possible Correct Answers: 10

Date _____   Your Correct Answers: _____

1. Stella did some perfect dives yesterday.

   She did 12 more perfect dives today than yesterday.

   n stands for the number of perfect dives she did yesterday.

   Which phrase shows today's number of perfect dives?

   (Circle the letter.)

   A. n x 12   B. n + 12   C. n – 12

2. Trixie swam for 70 minutes.

   Fuzzy swam a shorter time than Trixie.

   Which phrase shows the difference between the times? *(Circle the letter.)*

   A. 70 x n

   B. n + 70

   C. 70 – n

3. Which phrase means
   the sum of a number (n) and 57?
   (Circle the letter.)

   A. 57 – n

   B. 57 x n

   C. 57 + n

4. Which phrase means
   3 times the size of 50?
   (Circle the letter.)

   A. 50 + 3

   B. 50 – 3

   C. 50 x 3

5. Read the problem.

The dinosaurs had 22 new boats.

7 boats sprang a leak and sank.

How many boats were left?

Which number sentence can be used to find the number of boats left? *(Circle the letter.)*

A. $n - 22 = 7$ B. $22 - 7 = n$ C. $7 + 22 = n$

For problems 6–8, **n** stands for a number.
The same number is missing from each problem.
Write <, >, or = in each box.

6. $20 + n$ ☐ $20 - n$

7. $6 - n$ ☐ $3 + 3 - n$

8. $n + 10$ ☐ $10 + n$

9. If **n** stands for the number 5, what is the answer to this problem?

$14 - n =$ ☐

10. What is **n** in this problem?

$n \times 3 = 21$ $n =$ ☐

Name

Second Grade Book of Math Tests

Problem-Solving Process

Name _____   Possible Correct Answers: 20

Date _____   Your Correct Answers: _____

DIRECTIONS:

1) Choose ONE of the problems on the next page (page 2 of this test).

2) Use the space on pages 3 and 4 to solve the problem.

3) Show your answer and ALL your work clearly.
   Show any pictures or drawings you used to solve the problem.

4) After you get the answer, EXPLAIN how you found the answer.
   Write down the steps you followed to find the answer.

* Your problem solving will be scored on these four areas.
* You can receive 1 to 5 points for each one.

1) Your work shows that *you* understand the problem.

2) You chose a way to solve the problem that worked.

3) Your final answer is correct.

4) You used words and pictures or numbers to explain how
   you solved the problem.

Step # 1 Choose one problem.

Use the next 2 pages to solve the problem.
Show all your work and explain how you did the problem.

PROBLEM # 1

A runner gets ready for a race by running around this field.

She runs around the field twice.

How far will she run?

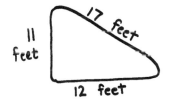

PROBLEM # 2

Dino and Ozzie are friends.
Dino is the oldest.
The sum of their ages is 23.
The difference between their ages is 5 years.
How old are they?

PROBLEM # 3

A player throws 6 sharp arrows at this target.

Five arrows have been thrown.

If this player is going to get 75 points, what will be the score of the last arrow?

PROBLEM # 4

Four carts are in a race.
Cart A is slower than Cart D.
Cart B is faster than Cart D.
Cart C is faster than Cart A.
Cart C does not win.
Which cart wins the race?

Name

Second Grade Book of Math Tests

Name _____   Problem # _____

Step # 2 Solve the problem.

You can use these two pages.
Show all your work. Show your answer.

_____

_____

_____

_____

_____

_____

_____

_____

_____

_____

_____

_____

_____

Second Grade Book of Math Tests

Name _____

Problem # _____

Step # 3 Explain how you solved the problem.

Explain this with words, pictures, numbers, or symbols.

_____

_____

_____

_____

_____

_____

_____

_____

_____

_____

_____

_____

_____

_____

* When you finish, review your work.
* Make sure you showed all your work.
* Make sure you showed your answer.
* Make sure you have explained how you solved the problem.

STOP

Geometry & Measurement
Skills Checklists

Geometry & Measurement Test # 1:

GEOMETRY

Test Location: pages 94–99

Skill	Test Items
Identify and name plane geometry figures	1–7
Identify angles and line segments	3, 4
Identify figures with curved lines	8, 13
Identify plane figures within illustrations	9–13
Identify congruent figures	14, 15
Identify similar figures	16
Recognize plane figures after they have been moved with a slide, flip, or turn	17–19
Recognize how a line segment can divide a figure to form other figures	20
Identify and name space figures	21–29
Identify figures that are symmetrical or that, when folded on a line, have symmetrical parts	30

Second Grade Book of Math Tests
Copyright ©2001 by Incentive Publications, Inc., Nashville, TN.

Geometry & Measurement Test # 2:

MEASUREMENT

Test Location: pages 100–105

Geometry & Measurement Test # 3:

TIME & TEMPERATURE

Test Location: pages 106–109

Geometry

Name _____   Possible Correct Answers: 30

Date _____   Your Correct Answers: _____

Look at the figures.
Write the letter of the figure that matches each word.

____ 1. square

____ 2. rectangle

____ 3. angle

____ 4. line segment

____ 5. hexagon

____ 6. triangle

____ 7. circle

8. Which shape has
   curved lines?

   Write the letter. _____

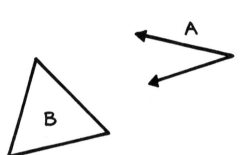
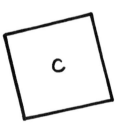
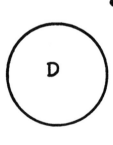
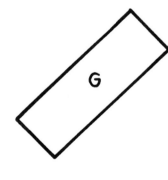

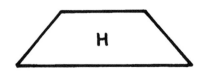

Second Grade Book of Math Tests

9. The sail on Fuzzy's boat is a shape with 4 sides.

   Which shape could this be?

   (Circle one answer.)

   A. circle   C. rectangle

   B. hexagon   D. triangle

---

10. The sail on Ty's boat is a shape with 3 sides.

    Which shape could this be?
    (Circle one answer.)

    A. square   C. rectangle

    B. hexagon   D. triangle

---

11. The sail on Rocky's boat is a shape with 4 sides.

    Which shape could this be?
    (Circle two answers.)

    A. square   C. rectangle

    B. hexagon   D. triangle

---

12. The sail on Brock's boat is a shape with 6 sides.

    Which shape could this be?

    (Circle one answer.)

    A. square   C. rectangle

    B. hexagon   D. triangle

13. The sail on Trixie's boat is a shape with curves.

    Which shape could this be?

    (Circle one answer.)

    A. circle   C. rectangle

    B. hexagon   D. triangle

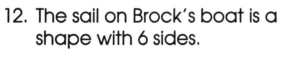

Name

    Second Grade Book of Math Tests

14. Circle the shape below that is
    the same size and shape as this one:

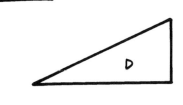

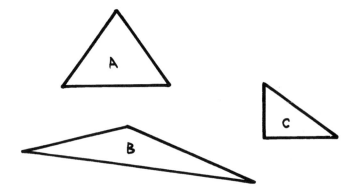

15. Circle the shape below that
    is the same size and shape as this one:

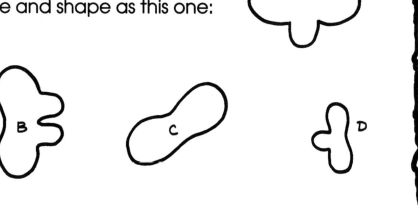

16. Circle the shape below
    that is the same shape as this one:

A. 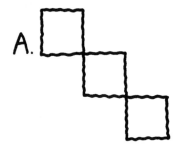   B. 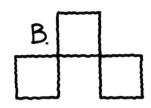   C.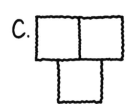

Name

96

17. Is A the same shape as B?
    (Circle yes or no.)

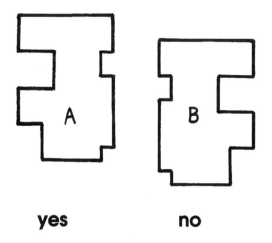

yes   **no**

18. Is C the same shape as D?
    (Circle yes or no.)

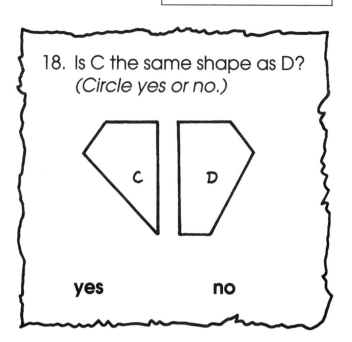

yes   **no**

19. Circle the shape that is the same shape as F.

   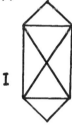 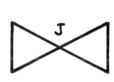

20. Which line segment divides this figure into 2 squares?

    (Circle one answer.)

    A. line segment AC

    B. line segment AF

    C. line segment BG

    D. line segment BE

    E. line segment AD

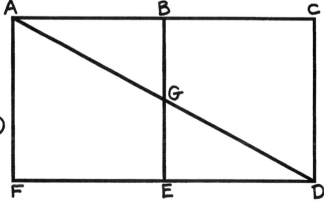

Name

Does Roxanne know the names of these space figures?

Look at her answers.

If an answer is correct, circle the number.

If an answer is not correct, cross it out and write the correct name.

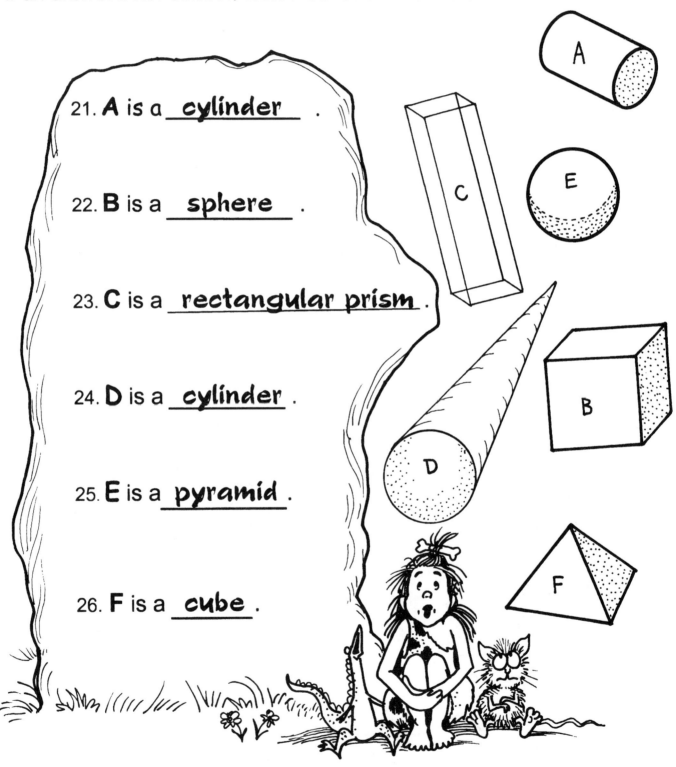

21. **A** is a __cylinder__ .

22. **B** is a __sphere__ .

23. **C** is a __rectangular prism__ .

24. **D** is a __cylinder__ .

25. **E** is a __pyramid__ .

26. **F** is a __cube__ .

Name

Second Grade Book of Math Tests   Copyright ©2001 by Incentive Publications, Inc., Nashville, TN.

27. Rocky's hat is one of these figures.

Which one is it? *(Circle one answer.)*

A. cone   B. rectangular prism   C. sphere

D. cylinder   E. cube

28. A can of soda pop is one of these figures.

Which one is it?
(Circle one answer.)
A. cone
B. sphere
C. rectangular prism
D. cylinder
E. cube

29. A tennis ball is one of these figures.

Which one is it?
(Circle one answer.)
A. cone
B. sphere
C. rectangular prism
D. cylinder
E. cube

30. Each shape below will be folded on the dotted line.

Some shapes will have both sides matching when they are folded. Circle those shapes.

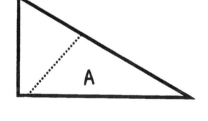

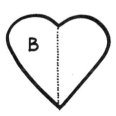

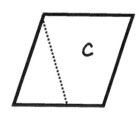

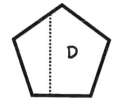

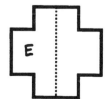

Name

Second Grade Book of Math Tests

Measurement

Name _____   Possible Correct Answers: 40

Date _____   Your Correct Answers: _____

Tell what each measurement unit is used to measure.
Choose one answer for each unit in problems 1–6.

1. a **cup** measures
   A. length
   B. weight
   C. the amount something holds

2. an **inch** measures
   A. length
   B. weight
   C. the amount something holds

3. a **gram** measures
   A. length
   B. weight
   C. the amount something holds

4. a **foot** measures
   A. length
   B. weight
   C. the amount something holds

5. a **liter** measures
   A. length
   B. weight
   C. the amount something holds

6. a **pound** measures
   A. length
   B. weight
   C. the amount something holds

7. Circle the one that holds more.

pint
A

quart
B

8. Circle the one that is heavier.

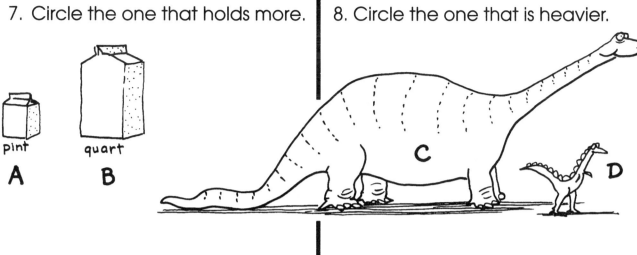

C

D

9. Circle the one that weighs about a gram.

A

B

10. Circle the one that holds about a liter.

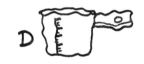

CAVE ROCK SODA
C

D

11. Circle the one that weighs about a kilogram.

A

B

12. Circle the one that would be about three inches long.

A. a math book
B. a lion's tail
C. a jump rope
D. your finger

Name

Second Grade Book of Math Tests

13. Which measurement is the best estimate for the amount of water shown? *(Circle the letter.)*

    A. 1 liter   B. 1 cup   C. 5,000 liters   D. 25 gallons

14. Brock walks 10 meters looking for some dinner.

    Fuzzy travels 10 feet looking for some dinner.

    Terra flies 10 miles looking for her dinner.

    Who travels the farthest?_____

15. Circle the largest unit:

    gram   kilogram

16. Circle the largest unit:

    quart   pint   gallon   cup

17. Circle the largest unit:

    foot   yard   inch   mile

18. Circle the largest unit:

    year   minute   hour   second

Name _____

Second Grade Book of Math Tests   Copyright ©2001 by Incentive Publications, Inc., Nashville, TN.

Do the measurements below make sense?
For each item (19–22), circle yes or no.

19. A dinosaur weighs 3 grams.

   yes   **no**

20. Rocky can run 200 miles an hour.

   yes   **no**

21. Five dinosaurs swim in a pool
    that holds 10 quarts of water.

   yes   **no**

22. Rocky kicks a rock 10 meters.

   yes   **no**

Circle the unit that would be the BEST one for Roxanne to use
when she measures each of these.

23. water in a glass	**cups**	**gallons**
24. water in a small pond	**pints**	**gallons**
25. weight of a bug	**ounces**	**pounds**
26. length of a ball game	**seconds**	**minutes**

Name

Circle the name of the tool that Rap should use to measure these:

27. the weight of a tree branch

   A. a ruler

   B. a scale

   C. a clock

   D. a gallon jug

28. the length of Brock's tail

   A. a liter bottle

   B. a thermometer

   C. a meter stick

   D. a scale

Fill in the missing measurements.

29. Stella swam 1 foot. How many inches? _____

30. Fuzzy is 12 months old. How many years? _____

31. Terra ate a pound of berries. How many ounces? _____

32. Roxanne jumped 1 meter. How many centimeters? _____

33. Ty drank a gallon of river water. How many quarts? _____

34. Trixie was lost for 24 hours.

   How many days? _____

35. A swimming camp was 2 weeks long.

   How many days? _____

36. A swimmer is 4 years old.

   How many months? _____

Name

Second Grade Book of Math Tests

37. About how long is this curved line?

    A. 1 inch

    B. $\frac{1}{2}$ inch

    C. 3 inches

    D. 6 inches

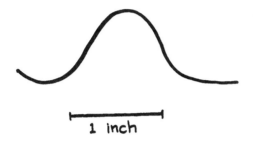

38. How tall is the dinosaur?

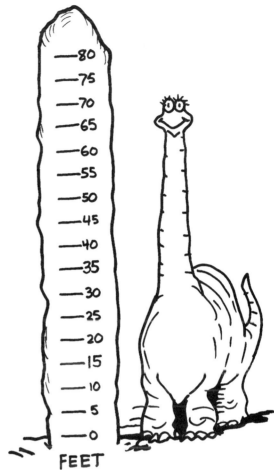

FEET

Answer: _____

39. Rocky found a nest full of eggs.
    He counted all of them.
    He counted 2 dozen eggs.
    How many eggs were in the nest?

    Answer: _____

40. Who drank more?

    A. a runner who drank 2 pints

    B. a runner who drank 2 quarts

    C. a runner who drank 2 gallons

    D. a runner who drank 2 liters

Name

Second Grade Book of Math Tests

Time & Temperature

Name _____   Possible Correct Answers: 20

Date _____   Your Correct Answers: _____

1. The water contests began at the time shown on the clock.

What time did they begin? _____

2. The contests ended at this time.
   What time did they end?

   _____

3. About how long did the contests last? _____

4. Brock got home late from
   the busy day at the river.

   The clock shows the time
   he got home.
   What time was it? _____

5. The back-floating contest started at 10:15 in the morning.

It ended 2 hours and 10 minutes later.

What time did it end?

A. 10:25
B. 12:15
C. 12:25
D. 6:00

6. The nose-holding contest lasted $1\frac{1}{2}$ hours.

It ended at 4:00.

What time did it start?

A. 1:30
B. 2:30
C. 3:30
D. 5:30

7. Read the time on clock A.

What time will it be in 20 minutes?

_____

8. Read the time on clock B.

What time was it 30 minutes ago?

_____

9. Read the time on clock C.

What time will it be in 45 minutes?

_____

Name

Second Grade Book of Math Tests

10. How many days are in a week? _____

11. How many hours are in a day? _____

12. How many minutes are in an hour? _____

13. What is the last month of the year? _____

14. What is the fifth month of the year? _____

Use the calendar for questions 15 and 16.

JULY						
Sun	Mon	Tue	Wed	Thurs	Fri	Sat
1	2 Swim Practice	3	4 Floating Practice	5	6	7
8	9	10 Floating Practice	11	12	13	14 Water Contest Day
15	16	17	18	19 Swim Practice	20	21
22	23 Floating Practice	24	25	26 Snorkel Lessons	27	28
29	30	31 Diving Contest				

15. What date is 2 weeks and 3 days after the Water Contest Day?

_____

16. What day of the week is July 16th?

_____

Name _____

Write the temperature shown on each thermometer.

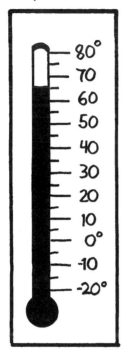 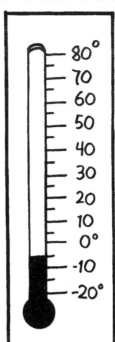 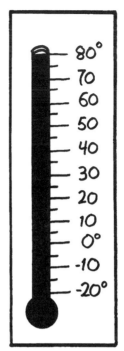

17. _____ °F   18. _____ °F   19. _____ °F

20. On the morning of the Water Contest Day,
the temperature was 55° F.

By the time the contests were over, the temperature had risen 38°.

What was the temperature when the contests ended?

A. 17° F

B. 93° F

C. 83° F

D. 27° F

Name

Second Grade Book of Math Tests

Graphing, Statistics, & Probability Skills Checklists

Graphing, Statistics, & Probability Test # 1:

COORDINATE GRAPHING

Test Location: pages 112–115

Skill	*Test Items*
Find the location of objects on a one-quadrant coordinate grid	1–4, 9–12
Write the coordinates of objects on a one-quadrant coordinate grid	5–8, 13–16

Graphing, Statistics, & Probability Test # 2:

PROBABILITY

Test Location: pages 116–117

Skill	*Test Items*
Use the words *more likely, most likely, less likely, least likely,* and *equally likely* to describe the chance of an event happening	1, 3, 6–10
Determine the number of possible outcomes of an event	2
Describe the probability of a particular outcome	4, 5

Second Grade Book of Math Tests

Graphing, Statistics, & Probability Test # 3:

STATISTICS & GRAPHS

Test Location: pages 118–124

Skill	Test Items
Read and interpret a frequency tally sheet	1–4
Read and interpret tables of data	5–12
Solve problems using data on a table	5, 8, 10–12
Read and interpret frequency tables	9–12
Read and interpret a bar graph	13–16
Solve problems using data on a bar graph	15, 16
Read and interpret a pictograph	17–21
Solve problems using data on a pictograph	19–21
Read and interpret a circle graph	22–25
Solve problems using data on a circle graph	24, 25
Read and interpret a line graph	26–30
Solve problems using data on a line graph	28, 30

Second Grade Book of Math Tests   Copyright ©2001 by Incentive Publications, Inc., Nashville, TN.

Coordinate Graphing

Name _____

Date _____

Possible Correct Answers: 16

Your Correct Answers: _____

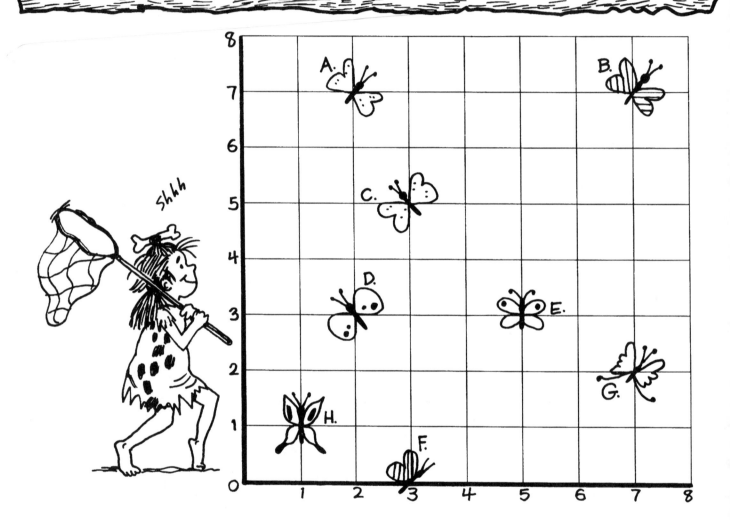

Roxanne is following butterflies.

They are scattered all over the grid.
Write the letter of the butterflies who are resting at each of these locations.

1. (5 over, 3 up) _____

2. (7 over, 2 up) _____

3. (7 over, 7 up) _____

4. (3 over, 0 up) _____

Second Grade Book of Math Tests

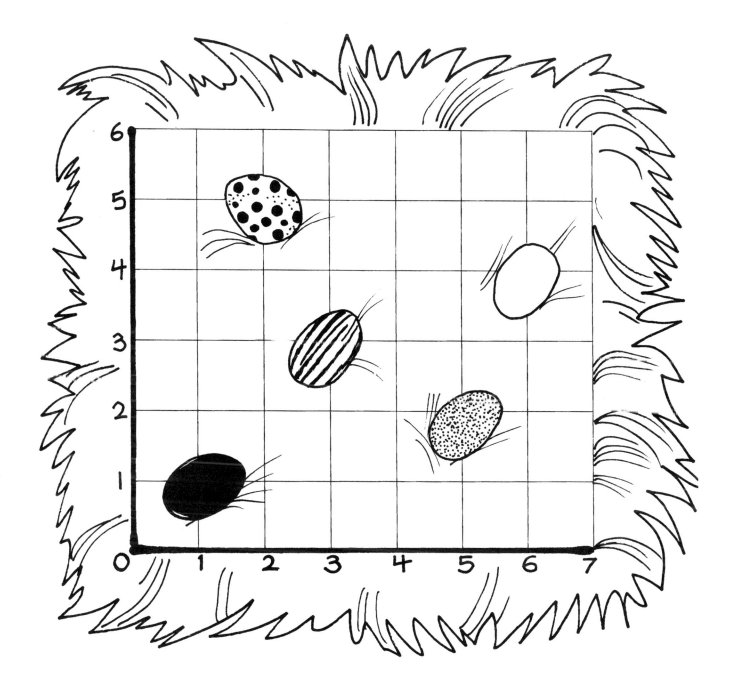

A nest of eggs has been found. Write the locations of these eggs.

Write the number over from 0 first, then the number up from 0.

5. The striped egg (_____ , _____)   7. The spotted egg (_____ , _____)

6. The white egg (_____ , _____)   8. The black egg (_____ , _____)

Name

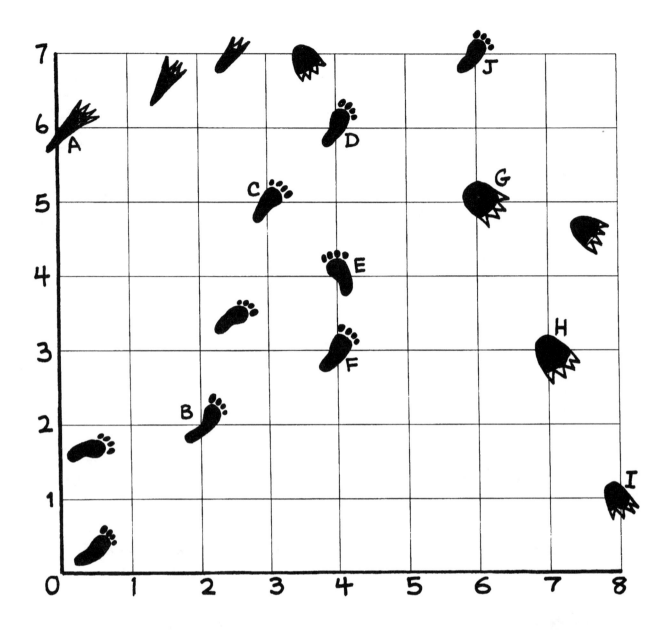

Write the letter of the footprint found at each location given below.

9. (0, 6) _____

10. (4, 4) _____

11. (6, 5) _____

12. (4, 6) _____

Name

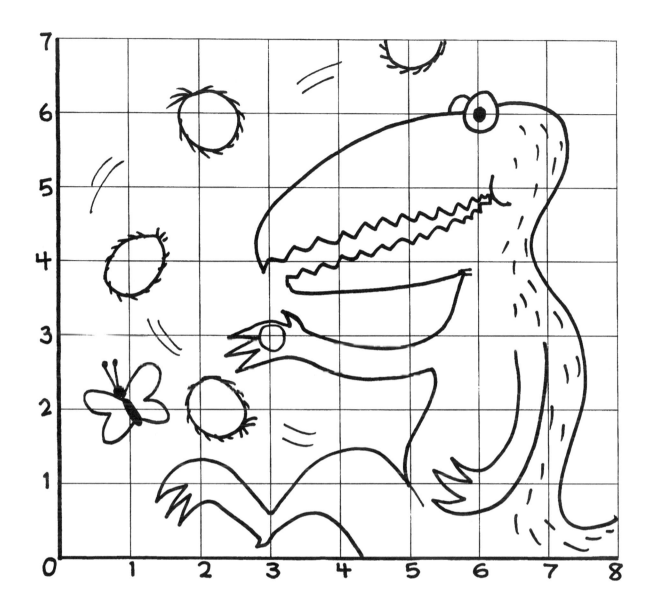

Answer the questions about this picture.

Write the locations like this: 5 over and 7 up = (5, 7)

13. Is there an eye at (6, 7)? _____

14. Is there a coconut at (4, 1)? _____

15. Where is the tip of Ty's nose? _____

16. Where is the butterfly? _____

Name

Second Grade Book of Math Tests

Probability

Name _____

Possible Correct Answers: 10

Date _____

Your Correct Answers: _____

1. Stella reaches into a pile of pebbles and grabs a pebble without seeing it.

   The pile has these pebbles: **5 blue, 7 speckled, 2 gray, 4 brown.**

   Which color pebble is she most likely to grab?

   A. gray   C. speckled

   B. blue   D. brown

The pebbles will be tossed at the target below.

2. How many different letter possibilities are there for landing spots?

   _____

3. Stella tossed one pebble. On which letter is it most likely to land?

   _____

4. Brock tossed one pebble.

   What is the chance it will land on B?

   _____ out of 9

5. Ty tossed one pebble.

   What is the chance it will land on D?

   _____ out of _____

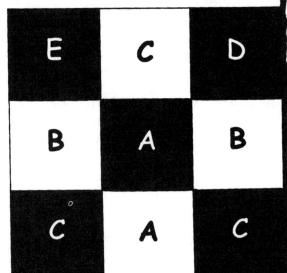

After the contest, the friends use the spinner to choose their snacks.
Brock spins the spinner once. You can see what his snack will be.
Now Stella will spin.

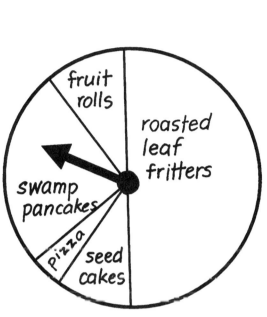

6. On which food is the spinner **most likely** to stop? _____

7. On which food is the spinner **least likely** to stop? _____

8. On which 2 foods is the spinner **equally likely** to stop?

_____ and _____

9. Which of these is **less likely**? *(Circle one.)*

     fruit rolls   *or*   swamp pancakes

10. Which of these is **more likely**? *(Circle one.)*

     pizza   *or*   roasted leaf fritters

Name

Second Grade Book of Math Tests

Statistics & Graphs

Name _____

Date _____

Possible Correct Answers: 30

Your Correct Answers: _____

SUMMER SPORTS

	Number Who Signed Up for the Sport	Number
Kickball	ⅢⅢ ⅢⅢ ⅢⅢ	15
Mudball Hitting	ⅢⅢ ⅢⅢ ⅢⅢ ⅢⅢ Ⅰ	21
Rock Lifting	ⅢⅢ ⅢⅢ ⅢⅢ ⅠⅠ	
Tail Wrestling	ⅢⅢ ⅠⅠⅠⅠ	9
Leaf Swallowing	ⅢⅢ ⅢⅢ ⅠⅠⅠⅠ	

Use Coach Ty's tally sheet for questions 1-4.

1. Which sport had the most members? _____

2. How many more signed up for rock-lifting than tail-wrestling? _____

3. Which two sports had about the same number of sign-ups?

_____

4. Which sport had 6 more than kickball? _____

Use the Kickball Scores chart for Questions 5–8.

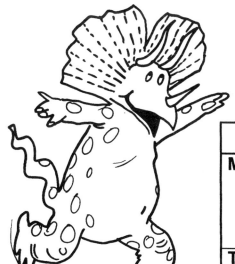

KICKBALL SCORES

Day	Teams	Scores
Monday	The Rock Kickers	25
	The Desert Champs	17
Tuesday	The Bigfoot Gang	18
	The Rock Kickers	20
Wednesday	The Bigfoot Gang	31
	The Desert Champs	30

5. What was the difference in scores at Monday's game?

_____ points

6. Which team won Wednesday's game? _____

7. Which team won the most games? _____

8. What is the difference between the highest and lowest scores on the chart?

_____ points

Name

Second Grade Book of Math Tests

The table below shows the medals won by The Rock City Team.

Use the table for questions 9–12.

9. How many gold medals were won in diving events?

_____

10. How many medals did the team win all together in pond-leaping?

_____

11. In which event did the team win the most medals (all colors together)?

_____

12. What was the total number of medals the team won in stone-skipping?

_____

MEDALS for POND EVENTS
Won by The Rock City Team

EVENTS	GOLD MEDALS	SILVER MEDALS	BRONZE MEDALS
Diving	6	2	3
Pond-Leaping	3	1	8
Stone-Skipping	4	0	4
Swimming	9	12	6

Name

Use the Rock-Lifting Records graph for questions 13–16.

13. Which team lifted about 90 pounds? _____

14. About how many pounds were lifted by the Strong Sisters?_____

15. About how many more pounds did the Boulder Brothers lift
    than the Hard Rock Twins? *(Circle the letter.)*

    A. 40 pounds   B. 70 pounds   C. 100 pounds

16. How many more pounds were lifted by the Mighty Dinos
    than the Strong Sisters? *(Circle the letter.)*

    A. 90 pounds   B. 60 pounds   C. 30 pounds

Name

Second Grade Book of Math Tests

Use the pictograph about the Mudball Games to answer questions 17–21.

17. Which team won 20 games? _____

18. How many games did Terra's team win? _____

19. How many more games did Rocky's team win than Ty's team? _____

20. Which team won 10 games fewer than Terra's team? _____

21. How many games were won by Stella's and Rocky's teams together?

    _____

The circle graph shows the number of leaves eaten in a contest.

Use the graph to answer questions 22–25.

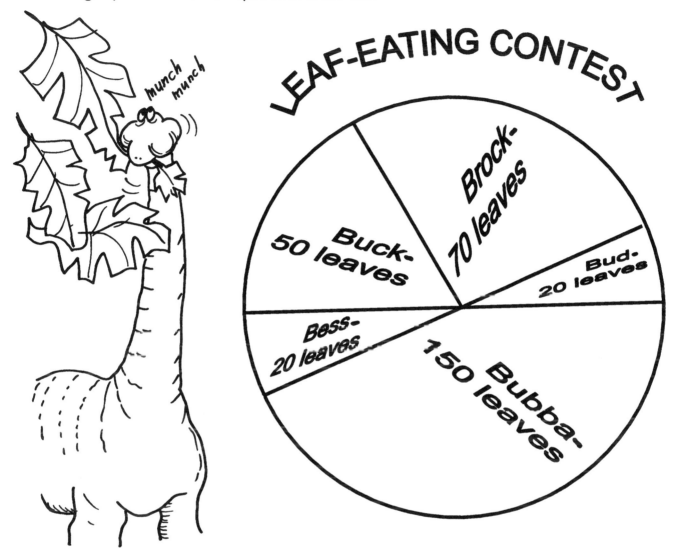

22. Who ate the most leaves? _____

23. Which two dinosaurs ate the same number of leaves?

_____ and _____

24. How many more leaves did Bubba eat than Brock? _____

25. How many leaves did Buck and Brock eat together? _____

Name

Second Grade Book of Math Tests

Brock practiced tail-wrestling every day for 8 weeks.

The graph shows how much time he practiced each week.

Use the graph for questions 26–30.

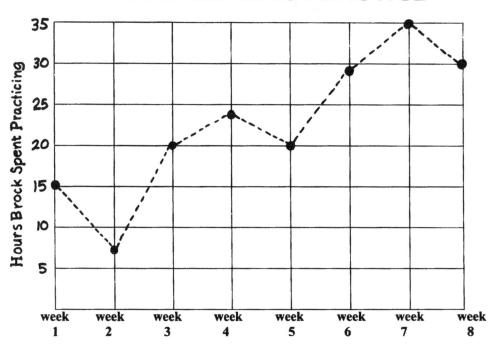

TAIL-WRESTLING PRACTICE

26. Which week did Brock practice 24 hours? _____

27. How many hours did he practice in week 3? _____

28. How much more did he practice in week 8 than week 5? _____

29. Did Brock's practice time increase every week? _____

30. What was the difference between his practice time in week 7 and week 1?

_____

Name

Keeping Track Of Skills

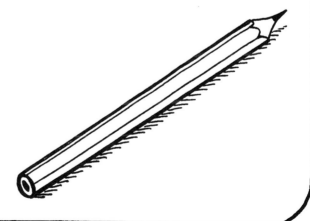

STUDENT PROGRESS RECORD FORM — MATH SKILLS

Student Name _____

TEST DATE	NUMBER CONCEPTS & RELATIONSHIPS TESTS	SCORE ___ OF ___	COMMENTS & NEEDS
	Test # 1 Counting	of 25	
	Test # 2 Reading & Writing Numbers	of 25	
	Test # 3 Number Concepts	of 30	
	Test # 4 Place Value	of 25	
	Test # 5 Number Relationships	of 25	

TEST DATE	COMPUTATION TESTS	SCORE ___ OF ___	COMMENTS & NEEDS
	Test # 1 Addition Facts	of 35	
	Test # 2 Addition with 2 and 3 Digits	of 20	
	Test # 3 Subtraction Facts	of 35	
	Test # 4 Subtraction with 2 and 3 Digits	of 25	
	Test # 5 Addition and Subtraction	of 25	
	Test # 6 Multiplication	of 30	

TEST DATE	FRACTIONS & MONEY TESTS	SCORE ___ OF ___	COMMENTS & NEEDS
	Test # 1 Fractions	of 30	
	Test # 2 Money	of 20	

TEST DATE	PROBLEM-SOLVING TESTS	SCORE ___ OF ___	COMMENTS & NEEDS
	Test # 1 Problem-Solving Strategies	of 15	
	Test # 2 Patterns	of 15	
	Test # 3 Problems to Solve	of 30	
	Test # 4 Algebra Concepts	of 10	
	Test # 5 Problem-Solving Process	of 20	

TEST DATE	GEOMETRY & MEASUREMENT TESTS	SCORE ___ OF ___	COMMENTS & NEEDS
	Test # 1 Geometry	of 30	
	Test # 2 Measurement	of 40	
	Test # 3 Time & Temperature	of 20	

TEST DATE	GRAPHING, STATISTICS, & PROBABILITY TESTS	SCORE ___ OF ___	COMMENTS & NEEDS
	Test # 1 Coordinate Graphing	of 16	
	Test # 2 Probability	of 10	
	Test # 3 Statistics & Graphs	of 30	

Second Grade Book of Math Tests   Copyright ©2001 by Incentive Publications, Inc., Nashville, TN.

CLASS PROGRESS RECORD — MATH SKILLS

Numbers Concepts & Relationships, Computation, and Fractions & Money

Class _____

Teacher _____

NUMBER CONCEPTS & RELATIONSHIPS TESTS

TEST DATE	TEST	COMMENTS ABOUT RESULTS	SKILLS NEEDING RE-TEACHING
	Test # 1 Counting		
	Test # 2 Reading & Writing Numbers		
	Test # 3 Number Concepts		
	Test # 4 Place Value		
	Test # 5 Number Relationships		

COMPUTATION TESTS

TEST DATE	TEST	COMMENTS ABOUT RESULTS	SKILLS NEEDING RE-TEACHING
	Test # 1 Addition Facts		
	Test # 2 Addition with 2 and 3 Digits		
	Test # 3 Subtraction Facts		
	Test # 4 Subtraction with 2 and 3 Digits		
	Test # 5 Addition & Subtraction		
	Test # 6 Multiplication		

FRACTIONS & MONEY TESTS

TEST DATE	TEST	COMMENTS ABOUT RESULTS	SKILLS NEEDING RE-TEACHING
	Test # 1 Fractions		
	Test # 2 Money		

Second Grade Book of Math Tests

CLASS PROGRESS RECORD — MATH SKILLS
Problem Solving, Geometry & Measurement, and Graphing, Statistics, & Probability

Class _____   Teacher _____

PROBLEM-SOLVING TESTS

TEST DATE	TEST	COMMENTS ABOUT RESULTS	SKILLS NEEDING RE-TEACHING
	Test # 1 Problem-Solving Strategies		
	Test # 2 Patterns		
	Test # 3 Problems to Solve		
	Test # 4 Algebra Concepts		
	Test # 5 Problem-Solving Process		

GEOMETRY & MEASUREMENT

TEST DATE	TEST	COMMENTS ABOUT RESULTS	SKILLS NEEDING RE-TEACHING
	Test # 1 Geometry		
	Test # 2 Measurement		
	Test # 3 Time & Temperature		

GRAPHING, STATISTICS, & PROBABILITY TESTS

TEST DATE	TEST	COMMENTS ABOUT RESULTS	SKILLS NEEDING RE-TEACHING
	Test # 1 Coordinate Graphing		
	Test # 2 Probability		
	Test # 3 Statistics & Graphs		

Second Grade Book of Math Tests   Copyright ©2001 by Incentive Publications, Inc., Nashville, TN.

GOOD SKILL SHARPENERS FOR MATH

The tests in this book will identify student needs for practice, re-teaching or reinforcement of basic skills. Once these areas of need are known, some good ways to strengthen those skills must be found.

The BASIC/Not Boring Skills Series, published by Incentive Publications (www.incentivepublications.com), offers 10 books to sharpen basic skills at the Grades 2-3 level. Three of the books are full of math exercises.

The pages of these books are student-friendly, clever, and challenging— guaranteed not to be boring! They cover a wide range of skills, including the skills assessed in this book of tests. A complete checklist of skills is available at the front of each book, complete with a reference list directing you to the precise pages for polishing those skills.

TEST IN THIS BOOK 2nd Grade Book of Math Tests	Pages in this Book	You will find pages to sharpen skills in these locations from the BASIC/Not Boring Skills Series, published by Incentive Publications.
Number Concepts & Relationships Test # 1 **Counting**	12–15	Gr. 2–3 Number Concepts & Relationships
Number Concepts & Relationships Test # 2 **Reading & Writing Numbers**	16–19	Gr. 2–3 Number Concepts & Relationships
Number Concepts & Relationships Test # 3 **Number Concepts**	20–23	Gr. 2–3 Number Concepts & Relationships Gr. 2–3 Math Computation & Problem Solving
Number Concepts & Relationships Test # 4 **Place Value**	24–27	Gr. 2–3 Number Concepts & Relationships Gr. 2–3 Math Computation & Problem Solving
Number Concepts & Relationships Test # 5 **Number Relationships**	28–31	Gr. 2–3 Number Concepts & Relationships Gr. 2–3 Math Computation & Problem Solving
Computation Test # 1 **Addition Facts**	34–39	Gr. 2–3 Math Computation & Problem Solving
Computation Test # 2 **Addition with 2 and 3 Digits**	40–43	Gr. 2–3 Math Computation & Problem Solving
Computation Test # 3 **Subtraction Facts**	44–47	Gr. 2–3 Math Computation & Problem Solving
Computation Test # 4 **Subtraction with 2 and 3 Digits**	48–51	Gr. 2–3 Math Computation & Problem Solving

GOOD SKILL SHARPENERS FOR MATH

TEST IN THIS BOOK 2nd Grade Book of Math Tests	Pages in this Book	You will find pages to sharpen skills in these locations from the BASIC/Not Boring Skills Series, published by Incentive Publications.
Computation Test # 5 **Addition and Subtraction**	52–55	Gr. 2–3 Math Computation & Problem Solving
Computation Test # 6 **Multiplication**	56–59	Gr. 2–3 Math Computation & Problem Solving
Fractions & Money Test # 1 **Fractions**	62–65	Gr. 2–3 Math Computation & Problem Solving Gr. 2–3 Number Concepts & Relationships
Fractions & Money Test # 2 **Money**	66–69	Gr. 2–3 Math Computation & Problem Solving Gr. 2–3 Number Concepts & Relationships
Problem-Solving Test # 1 **Problem-Solving Strategies**	72–75	Gr. 2–3 Math Computation & Problem Solving
Problem-Solving Test # 2 **Patterns**	76–79	Gr. 2–3 Math Computation & Problem Solving
Problem-Solving Test # 3 **Problems to Solve**	80–85	Gr. 2–3 Math Computation & Problem Solving
Problem-Solving Test # 4 **Algebra Concepts**	86–87	Gr. 2–3 Math Computation & Problem Solving
Problem-Solving Test # 5 **Problem-Solving Process**	88–91	Gr. 2–3 Math Computation & Problem Solving
Geometry & Measurement Test # 1 **Geometry**	94–99	Gr. 2–3 Geometry & Measurement
Geometry & Measurement Test # 2 **Measurement**	100–105	Gr. 2–3 Geometry & Measurement
Geometry & Measurement Test # 3 **Time & Temperature**	106–109	Gr. 2–3 Geometry & Measurement Gr. 2–3 Math Computation & Problem Solving
Graphing, Statistics, & Probability Test # 1 **Coordinate Graphing**	112–115	Gr. 2–3 Math Computation & Problem Solving
Graphing, Statistics, & Probability Test # 2 **Probability**	116–117	Gr. 2–3 Math Computation & Problem Solving
Graphing, Statistics, & Probability Tests # 3 **Statistics & Graphs**	118–124	Gr. 2–3 Math Computation & Problem Solving

Scoring Guide & Answer Keys

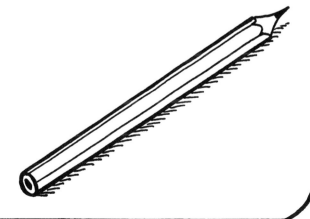

Number Concepts & Relationships
Answer Key

Counting
(Test on page 12)

1. fourth	11. 63	19. 98, 96, 94, 92
2. yes	12. 107	20. 30, 40, 45
3. no	13. 30	21. 80, 75, 70, 65
4. Trixie	14. 120	22. 80, 100, 110, 120
5. first	15. 76	
6. seventh	16–24: The missing numbers are:	23. 300, 400, 500, 600
7. Stella		24. 240, 220, 210, 200
8. Ty	16. 99, 100, 101	
9. 17	17. 252, 249	25. 20
10. 38	18. 88, 90, 92	

Reading & Writing Numbers
(Test on page 16)

1. 22	14. B
2. 86	15. E
3. 103	16. one thousand
4. $\frac{1}{2}$	17. sixteen
5. 220	18. sixty-five
6. 67¢	19. five hundred fifty
7. 14	20. ninety-nine
8. 40	21. three hundred
9. 142	22. B
10. 780	23. A
11. 869	24. D
12. 1,256	25. C
13. B	

Number Concepts & Relationships
Answer Key

Number Concepts
(Test on page 20)

1. 6, 12, 5000, 100, 44, 60
2. 3, 81, 13, 77, 9, 7, 11, 55
3. B
4. A
5. C
6. 8
7. 6
8. 5
9. C
10. 30
11. 10
12. 80
13. 40
14. 30
15. 90
16. 60
17. 60
18. 300
19. 500
20. 900
21. 700
22. 600
23. 300
24. Rocky
25. Stella
26. Ty
27. Brock
28. Terra
29. Fuzzy
30. Trixie

Place Value
(Test on page 24)

1. 162
2. 68
3. 594
4. 8,300
5. tens
6. hundreds
7. thousands
8. ones
9. A
10. C
11. 16,304
12–21: *Answers will vary. Make sure student writes a number that meets the specifications.*
12. 4 in the tens place
13. 6 in the hundreds place
14. 3 in the ones place
15. 2 in the thousands place
16. 3 digits with 0 in the ones place
17. 3 digits with 7 in the tens place
18. 4 digits with 5 in the hundreds place
19. 4 digits with 0 in the tens place
20. 3 digits with 9 in the tens place
21. 3 digits with 8 in the ones place
22. Rock Champs
23. 100 Pound Club
24. Bold Boulders
25. Tough Guys

Second Grade Book of Math Tests

Number Concepts & Relationships
Answer Key

Number Relationships
(Test on page 28)

1. B
2. C
3. E
4. 66
5. 898
6. less than
7. less than
8. greater than
9. greater than
10. greater than
11. =
12. <
13. <
14. >
15. 196, 199, 204, 216, 228, 250
16. $ .65, $2.40, $3.05, $3.50, $4.20
17. 17, 42, 46, 970, 1700
18. C
19. 436
20. 810
21. 50
22. 500
23–25: There should be an X on 23 and 24; no X on 25.

Second Grade Book of Math Tests

Computation
Answer Key

Addition Facts
(Test on page 34)

1–15. The correct problems are 1, 4, 5, 8, 10, 13, 14	20. 13	28. 15
	21. 8	29. 3
	22. 12	30. 8
	23. 14	31. 15
16. 13	24. 16	32. 15
17. 18	25. 11	33. 6, 7, 4, 8
18. 15	26. 8	34. 4, 8, 7, 10
19. 14	27. 12	35. 18

Addition with 2 and 3 Digits
(Test on page 40)

1. Both problems	6. 61, 13 answer: 74	13. 91
2. Neither problem	7. 29, 32, 88 answer: 149	14. 72
3. Problem F		15. 369
4. 50, 32 answer: B	8. 55	16. 1016
	9. 16	17. D
5. 46, 29 answer: A	10. 59	18. 60
	11. 63	19. 40
	12. 30	20. 500

Subtraction Facts
(Test on page 44)

1–15. The correct problems are 4, 5, 6, 8, 9, 11, 12, 14	20. 6	28. 8
	21. 9	29. 10
	22. 7	30. 10
	23. 4	31. 0
16. 9	24. 7	32. 5
17. 7	25. 4	33. A
18. 8	26. 5	34. A
19. 9	27. 7	35. 15

Second Grade Book of Math Tests

Computation
Answer Key

Subtraction with 2 and 3 Digits
(Test on page 48)

1. Neither answer	10. 40	19. 60
2. Both answers	11. 93	20. 70
3. Both answers	12. 0	21. 0
4. $43; answer: C	13. 70	22. 50
5. $59, answer: $33	14. 58	23. 300
6. $72, answer: $36	15. 21	24. 90
7. $18	16. 25	25. 30
8. 56	17. A	
9. 30	18. A	

Addition & Subtraction
(Test on page 52)

1. 3, 8, 11, 11	10. +, +	19. yes
2. 8, 8, 7, 7	11. +	20. 17
3. 9, 8, 8, 9	12. +, +	21. 13
4. 9, 9, 12, 12	13. C	22. 20
5. B	14. 51 quarts	23. 0
6. A	15. 18	24. 620
7. +	16. 124	25. Rocky & Roxanne
8. –	17. 631	
9. –	18. no	

Multiplication
(Test on page 56)

1. 6	9. 50	17. 12	25. 80¢
2. 15	10. 6	18. 6	26. 20¢
3. 14	11. 14	19. 3	27. 18¢
4. 16	12. 30	20. 2	28. A
5. 9	13. 24	21. 3	29. A
6. 12	14. 21	22. 5	30. B
7. 30	15. 25	23. 3	
8. 0	16. 16	24. 21¢	

Second Grade Book of Math Tests　　　Copyright ©2001 by Incentive Publications, Inc., Nashville, TN.

Fractions & Money
Answer Key

Fractions
(Test on page 62)

1. $\frac{4}{9}$
2. $\frac{3}{9}$ (or $\frac{1}{3}$)
3. $\frac{1}{9}$
4. $\frac{2}{9}$
5. $\frac{1}{2}$
6. $\frac{2}{3}$
7. $\frac{1}{4}$
8. $\frac{4}{6}$ (or $\frac{2}{3}$)
9. $\frac{2}{5}$
10. $\frac{6}{10}$ (or $\frac{3}{5}$)
11. B, D, and F
12. L and E
13. K and G
14. C
15. $\frac{1}{3}$

16. $\frac{3}{4}$
17. $\frac{5}{6}$
18. $\frac{1}{2}$
19. B
20. Circle 2 dimes and 1 nickel
21. A
22. D
23. $\frac{1}{6}$
24. $\frac{6}{8}$
25. $1\frac{1}{6}$
26. $5\frac{2}{3}$
27. $6\frac{2}{10}$ (or $6\frac{1}{5}$)
28. $\frac{3}{5}$
29. $\frac{3}{6}$ (or $\frac{1}{2}$)
30. Ty

Money
(Test on page 66)

1.	66¢	8.	Brock	15.	<
2.	60¢	9.	$ 2.73	16.	>
3.	43¢	10.	40¢	17.	$ 7.00
4.	72¢	11.	57¢	18.	$ .17
5.	B	12.	B	19.	45¢
6.	B	13.	=	20.	no
7.	C	14.	<		

Second Grade Book of Math Tests

Problem-Solving
Answer Key

Problem-Solving Strategies
(Test on page 72)

1. no
2. yes
3. B
4. Cross out: 596 fans watched the swimming races.
5. B
6. C
7. A
8. C
9. 16
10. A
11. C
12. Dino
13. A. 7
    B. 9
14. A. 25
    B. 13
15. D

Patterns
(Test on page 76)

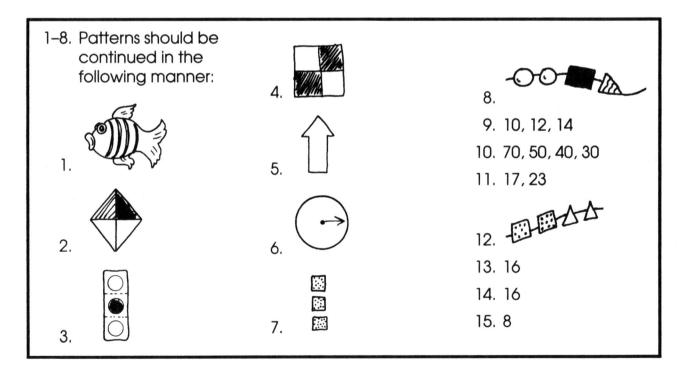

1–8. Patterns should be continued in the following manner:

1.
2.
3.
4.
5.
6.
7.
8.
9. 10, 12, 14
10. 70, 50, 40, 30
11. 17, 23
12.
13. 16
14. 16
15. 8

Problem-Solving
Answer Key

Problems to Solve
(Test on page 80)

1. B; 200	11. 2:30	21. 46 miles
2. 32 times	12. 4:30	22. 3
3. 97 minutes	13. 6, 7, 11	23. 11
4. 3	14. 2, 6	24. 2
5. 29	15. 4, 5, 10, 6, 11, 7	25. Rap
6. Trixie	16. 2	26. Brock
7. B	17. April 5	27. 200 meters
8. 6¢	18. April 22	28. $23.80
9. 101¢ or $1.01	19. 42 feet	29. 80 meters
10. 1:00	20. 8	30. 370 meters

Algebra Concepts
(Test on page 86)

1. B	6. >
2. C	7. =
3. C	8. =
4. C	9. 9
5. B	10. 7

Problem-Solving Process
(Test on page 88)

Teachers: Score student problems using the Problem-Solving Process Scoring Guide found on the next page (page 140). For accuracy, check problems with these answers:

1. 80 feet
2. Dino is 14; Ozzie is 9
3. 15 points
4. Cart B

Second Grade Book of Math Tests

PROBLEM-SOLVING PROCESS SCORING GUIDE

TRAIT	SCORE OF 5	SCORE OF 3	SCORE OF 1
UNDERSTANDING THE PROBLEM	• Student's work shows that the problem is clearly identified and understood. • Student's work shows that the student has done an excellent job of changing the written problem into a mathematical task.	• Student's work adequately shows that the problem is clearly identified and understood. • Student's work shows that the student has done an adequate job of changing the written problem into a mathematical task.	• Student's work does not show a clear identification or understanding of the problem. • Student's work shows that the student has only done a partial or an incorrect job of changing the written problem into a mathematical task.
STRATEGIES & PROCESSES	• Student has chosen one or more strategies that are appropriate to the problem. • The strategies have been used in a clear and complex manner. • The diagrams, pictures, models, or symbols that the student has used are clear and complete.	• Student has chosen one or more strategies that are appropriate to the problem. • The strategies have been used in a fairly clear and complete manner. • The diagrams, pictures, models, or symbols that the student has used are mostly complete and are relatively clear.	• Student has not chosen appropriate strategies, or has chosen appropriate strategies but has not used them correctly. • The diagrams, pictures, models, or symbols that the student has used are incomplete or do not lead to the solution.
COMMUNICATING THE WORK	• The student has used words, diagrams, pictures, models, numbers, and/or symbols to clearly show the steps taken toward a solution. • The student's explanation of the process used is a sensible and clear one.	• The student has used words, diagrams, pictures, models, numbers, and/or symbols to adequately show the steps taken toward a solution, but has not shown them in a complex or completely clear way. • The student's explanation of the process used is mostly sensible and clear.	• The student has not adequately used words, diagrams, pictures, models, numbers, and/or symbols to show the steps taken toward a solution. • The student's explanation of the process is sketchy, or nonexistent.
CORRECTNESS (Accuracy of the Answer)	• The student's answer is correct. • The student's work supports the answer that is given.	• The student's answer is mostly correct, with only minor errors. • The student's work supports the answer that is given.	• The student's answer is incomplete or incorrect. and/or • The student's work does not support the answer given.

A score of 4 may be given for work that falls between 3 and 5 on any given trait. A score of 2 may be given for work that falls between 1 and 3.

Second Grade Book of Math Tests

Geometry & Measurement
Answer Key

Geometry
(Test on page 94)

1. C	16. B
2. G or C	17. yes
3. A	18. no
4. E	19. H
5. F	20. D
6. B	21. Correct
7. D	22. cube
8. D	23. Correct
9. C	24. cone
10. D	25. sphere
11. A and C	26. pyramid
12. B	27. A
13. A	28. D
14. C	29. B
15. A	30. B, E, and F

Second Grade Book of Math Tests

Geometry & Measurement
Answer Key

Measurement
(Test on page 100)

1. C	15. kilogram	29. 12
2. A	16. gallon	30. 1
3. B	17. mile	31. 16
4. A	18. year	32. 100
5. C	19. no	33. 4
6. B	20. no	34. 1
7. B	21. no	35. 14
8. C	22. yes	36. 48
9. B	23. cups	37. C
10. C	24. gallons	38. 70 feet
11. A	25. ounces	39. 24
12. D	26. minutes	40. C
13. A	27. B	
14. Terra	28. C	

Time & Temperature
(Test on page 106)

1. 8:15	7. 5:30	14. May
2. 4:30	8. 12:30	15. July 31
3. 8 hours and 15 minutes or 81/4 hours	9. 8:00	16. Monday
	10. 7	17. 65°
4. 10:35	11. 24	18. −5°
5. C	12. 60	19. 80°
6. B	13. December	20. B

Second Grade Book of Math Tests   Copyright ©2001 by Incentive Publications, Inc., Nashville, TN.

Graphing, Statistics, & Probability Answer Key

Coordinate Graphing
(Test on page 112)

1. E
2. G
3. B
4. F
5. (3, 3)
6. (6, 4)
7. (2, 5)
8. (1, 1)
9. A
10. E
11. G
12. D
13. no
14. no
15. (3, 4)
16. (1, 2)

Probability
(Test on page 116)

1. C
2. 5
3. C
4. 2
5. 1 out of 9
6. roasted leaf fritters
7. pizza
8. fruit rolls and seed cakes
9. fruit rolls
10. fritters

Statistics & Graphs
(Test on page 118)

1. mudball hitting
2. 8
3. kickball and leaf swallowing
4. mudball hitting
5. 8
6. The Bigfoot Gang
7. The Rock Kickers
8. 14
9. 6
10. 12
11. swimming
12. 8
13. Hard Rock Twins
14. 120
15. B
16. C
17. Stella's
18. 30
19. 10
20. Stella's
21. 45
22. Bubba
23. Bess and Bud
24. 80 leaves
25. 120
26. 4
27. 20
28. 10 hours
29. no
30. 20 hours